D1391499

Mark Hix on Baking

Quadrille
PUBLISHING

CONTENTS

INTRODUCTION

It may sound strange, but whenever the word baking is mentioned around most of the cooks I know, they run a mile. Even those with lots of culinary experience can be terrified at the thought of cooking with precisely weighed out ingredients and having to follow the rigid rules of the pastry kitchen.

The funny thing is, baking doesn't have to be like this. Why? Well, firstly, baking is not just about cakes – it covers a wide range of savoury as well as sweet dishes too. Though most people associate it solely with cakes and pastry, piles of scones and sponges, afternoon tea and fancy patisserie, actually anything that has been cooked in the dry heat of an oven can be considered to be baked. Secondly, and most importantly, anyone can bake. Yes, a sophisticated soufflé does sound like a difficult undertaking (though it isn't as hard as many people believe) but a basic, filled baked potato is a simple yet delicious luxury that absolutely anyone can make, no matter how much experience they have in the kitchen.

Baking has always been an essential cooking method all over the world. Indeed, before stove tops and hobs were around, baking food in a natural, wood-fired oven would once have been the only way to cook anything, with the exception of cooking in a hole in the ground, perhaps. Ironically today a wood-fired oven is seen as a trendy, sophisticated luxury – one which only real foodies can be bothered to build in their gardens. Well, I'm a real foodie, I have a wood-fired oven and all I can say is that it produces simple food with the most fantastic flavours! But then again any oven, whether wood-fired, steam-injected or fan-assisted, can give great results – concentrating flavours, transforming textures and delivering exceptional food.

This book contains a selection of my favourite baked dishes, those which I have been cooking for years or have eaten on my travels around the globe. Some are exceptionally simple and quick to make, others take a little more time and effort. None of them are difficult, yet all of them, I think, are delicious. I hope you enjoy baking and eating your way through them.

SNACKS

Moroccan cigars

Preheat the oven to 220°C/gas mark 7.

Heat the oil in a heavy-based saucepan and fry the shallots, garlic and lamb on a high heat for 3–4 minutes, seasoning as it is cooking, until the meat starts to colour. Add the cinnamon and cumin and continue cooking for a minute. Add the stock and simmer for about 30 minutes, until the liquid has almost evaporated. Drain and roughly chop the raisins, add to the lamb with the pine nuts and continue simmering for a few minutes until the liquid has completely evaporated. Remove from the heat, season and leave to cool.

Cut the pastry into 6 x 8cm strips. Taking one strip, place a heaped teaspoon of the mix along the shorter edge nearest you. Brush the rest of the pastry lightly with butter and roll into a cigar shape as tightly as possible. Repeat with the remaining pastry strips, ensuring you cover the pastry you are not rolling with a damp cloth to prevent it drying up. Place the rolls on a lightly buttered baking tray a couple of centimetres apart and brush with butter.

Bake the cigars for about 8–10 minutes until golden and crisp. Dust with a little cinnamon and caster sugar and serve.

MAKES ABOUT 20

2–3 TBSP VEGETABLE OR CORN OIL

2 MEDIUM SHALLOTS, PEELED, HALVED AND FINELY CHOPPED

1 GARLIC CLOVE, PEELED AND CRUSHED

150G MINCED LAMB

SALT AND FRESHLY GROUND BLACK PEPPER

½ TSP GROUND CINNAMON, PLUS EXTRA FOR DUSTING

1 TSP GROUND CUMIN

150ML BEEF OR LAMB STOCK

1 TBSP RAISINS, SOAKED IN HOT WATER FOR AN HOUR

1 TBSP PINE NUTS, LIGHTLY TOASTED

150–200G READY-MADE WARKA OR FILO PASTRY (ABOUT 10–15 SHEETS)

50–60G BUTTER, MELTED

CASTER SUGAR, FOR DUSTING

- -

I've been making these tasty, neat little snacks for years now and serving them as appetisers or canapés with drinks. My chefs used to go nuts when a party ordered these as they take some time and patience to make, though they are well worth the effort. Traditionally warka pastry would be used for this dish, but filo pastry works just as well.

- -

Grissini

Preheat the oven to 180°C/gas mark 4.

Divide your dough into three equal-sized pieces. Mix one third with the Parmesan and one third with the rosemary, leaving the remaining third plain. Alternatively, keep the dough in one piece, combine the rosemary and Parmesan together in a bowl and add to the dough.

Take small balls of the dough and knead them on a lightly floured table for a minute or so. Roll them into long, thin sticks, about 20–30cm in length, starting with both your hands in the centre of the dough and moving them apart as you are rolling. (It takes a few to get the hang of it.)

Transfer the grissini to a lightly oiled baking tray. Dust the Parmesan ones with more Parmesan and the plain ones with a little polenta, if you like. Leave to stand for 15 minutes.

Bake for about 15 minutes, or until lightly coloured and crisp. Remove the grissini from the oven and store in an airtight container for up to 2–3 days. Serve as they are or warm through in a low oven before serving.

MAKES ABOUT 30

1 X PIZZA DOUGH WITH ONE PROVE (SEE PAGE 32)

160G FINELY GRATED PARMESAN, PLUS EXTRA FOR DUSTING

4 TBSP FINELY CHOPPED ROSEMARY NEEDLES

FLOUR, FOR DUSTING

FINE POLENTA, FOR DUSTING

- -

Grissini are great little snacks but the thought of making them – rolling loads of pencil-like sticks of dough – can initially seem daunting. Once you get the hang of the rolling technique however, the process becomes quite therapeutic and satisfying. I like to flavour mine with a few simple ingredients like Parmesan and rosemary but don't go too mad, as a good delicate grissini is a great snack in its own right.

- -

Dhal puffs

To make the dhal, melt the butter or ghee in a pan and gently cook the onion, garlic, chilli and spices for 3–4 minutes without colouring. Drain and rinse the peas and add to the pan with the stock. Season and simmer gently for about 30–40 minutes, stirring every so often, until the peas are cooked and tender, the liquid has been absorbed and the consistency is risotto-like. Stir in the coriander and leave to cool.

Preheat the oven to 220°C/gas mark 7.

On a lightly floured table, roll the dough out to about 3mm thick. Leave it to rest on the table for 5 minutes before cutting into roughly 4–5cm discs. Put a teaspoon of the dhal into the centre of each, brush the edges with water then bring the edges together to make a ball, reshaping them if necessary. Place them on a lightly oiled baking tray with the join side down and make a small slit in the top with the point of a small knife to expose the dhal. Brush with melted butter and scatter over the mustard and cumin seeds. Bake for about 12–15 minutes, or until golden. Serve warm.

SERVES 6–8

80G BUTTER OR GHEE

2 MEDIUM ONIONS, PEELED, HALVED AND FINELY CHOPPED

4 GARLIC CLOVES, PEELED AND CRUSHED

1 GREEN CHILLI, TRIMMED AND FINELY CHOPPED

1 TSP CUMIN SEEDS

1 TSP GROUND CUMIN

1 TSP BLACK MUSTARD SEEDS

1 TSP FENUGREEK SEEDS

1 TSP GROUND TURMERIC

10 CURRY LEAVES

150G CHANA DHAL (YELLOW DRIED) SPLIT PEAS, SOAKED FOR 2 HOURS IN COLD WATER

350ML VEGETABLE STOCK

3–4 TBSP CHOPPED CORIANDER

½ X PIZZA DOUGH WITH ONE PROVE (SEE PAGE 32)

FOR THE TOPPING

80G BUTTER, MELTED

1–2 TSP BLACK MUSTARD SEEDS

1–2 TSP CUMIN SEEDS

```
These delicious little bread-based
snacks are relatively quick to make
as you don't have to worry about
them proving a second time round.
Freeze them either uncooked or
lightly cooked and finish them off
in the oven for an emergency snack
moment or party.
```

Sausage rolls

Preheat the oven to 200°C/gas mark 6

Roll out the pastry on a floured table to about 3mm thick, then cut into 3mm wide strips. Wrap the pastry around the sausages leaving a gap about the width of the pastry and keeping the ends on one side of the sausage (i.e. the underneath when cooking). Place the sausages on a baking tray and brush the pastry with the beaten egg. Bake for about 20 minutes, or until the pastry is golden.

SERVES 8

200G READY-MADE ALL-BUTTER PUFF PASTRY

8 MINI COOKING CHORIZO, MORCILLA OR GOOD-QUALITY PORK SAUSAGES

1 EGG, BEATEN

- - - - - - - - - - - - - - - -
Sausage rolls don't have to be those bland, boring, ready-cooked things from the supermarket that get dished up at children's parties. When made with good-quality, interesting sausages such as cooking chorizo or black pudding they make great snacks for munching.
- - - - - - - - - - - - - - - -

Baked jumbo garlic with parsley salad

Preheat the oven to 200°C/gas mark 6.

Cut the tops off the heads of garlic about 1cm from the top. Replace the tops, wrap each head individually in foil and bake in the oven for 45 minutes, or until the garlic is soft.

Meantime, make the salad. Toss the parsley, capers and shallots in the vinegar, mustard and oil, season with salt and pepper and transfer to a small bowl.

Brush the slices of bread with a little olive oil and toast them on both sides. Place the garlic heads on a serving dish or board with the salad and toasts, along with teaspoons for your guests to scoop out the soft garlic and spread it onto the warm toasts.

SERVES 4–6

4 HEADS OF JUMBO OR ELEPHANT GARLIC

10–12 SLICES OF CIABATTA OR SOURDOUGH BREAD

EXTRA VIRGIN OLIVE OIL FOR BRUSHING

FOR THE PARSLEY SALAD

A COUPLE OF HANDFULS OF FLAT-LEAF PARSLEY LEAVES, WASHED AND DRIED

2 TBSP LARGE CAPERS, RINSED

2–3 MEDIUM SHALLOTS, PEELED, HALVED AND THINLY SLICED

½ TBSP WHITE WINE VINEGAR

1 TSP DIJON MUSTARD

1 TBSP EXTRA VIRGIN OLIVE OIL MIXED WITH 1 TBSP VEGETABLE OR CORN OIL

SALT AND FRESHLY GROUND BLACK PEPPER

- - - - - - - - - - - - - - - - - -
You occasionally see these super-sized jumbo or elephant garlic bulbs in supermarkets, specialist greengrocers and Asian shops. Baked in foil in the oven and served with some toasted ciabatta-type bread and a flat-leaf parsley salad they make a great snack to go on the dinner table.
- - - - - - - - - - - - - - - - - -

Baked bone marrow with oysters

Preheat the oven to 200°C/gas mark 6.

Gently cook the shallots and garlic in the butter for 2–3 minutes until soft, then remove from the heat.

Scoop the marrow out of the bones with a spoon and chop into rough pieces. Mix with the oysters, shallot mixture, breadcrumbs and parsley, and season. Spoon the mixture back into the bones, place on a baking tray and bake for about 12–15 minutes, until lightly coloured.

Serve in the middle of the table, with the toasted bread and teaspoons for sharing.

SERVES 4

4 SMALL SHALLOTS, PEELED, HALVED AND FINELY CHOPPED

2 GARLIC CLOVES, PEELED AND CRUSHED

A COUPLE OF GOOD KNOBS OF BUTTER

2 X 10–12CM HALVED BONE MARROW LENGTHS

8 ROCK OYSTERS, OPENED (SEE PAGE 112) AND CUT INTO 3

50–60G FRESH WHITE BREADCRUMBS

4 TBSP CHOPPED PARSLEY

SALT AND FRESHLY GROUND BLACK PEPPER

1 SMALL BAGUETTE, CUT INTO SLICES ON THE ANGLE AND TOASTED

- - - - - - - - - - - - - - - - - -

This is one of those dishes that came out of nowhere after my friend Dave visited the restaurant on a date and commented on how good the bone marrow and oysters were. Though he never actually ate the two things together, I thought it might not be a bad idea to try incorporating the oysters into the baked stuffed bone marrow — this great sharing dish is the result.

- - - - - - - - - - - - - - - - - -

Olive and cheese straws

Preheat the oven to 180°C/gas mark 4.

Roll the puff pastry out on a floured surface into a rectangle about 2–3mm thick and 10cm wide. Lay it on a baking tray, spread with half the tapenade and scatter over half of the cheese, then fold the pastry over. Spread the rest of the tapenade on the top and scatter over the chopped black olives and remaining cheese.

Bake for 15 minutes or until lightly coloured. Remove from the oven, transfer to a chopping board and cut into roughly 1cm wide fingers. Serve warm.

SERVES 6–8

200G READY-MADE ALL-BUTTER PUFF PASTRY

60–80G GREEN OLIVE TAPENADE

60G FINELY GRATED PARMESAN

8–10 STONED BLACK OLIVES, ROUGHLY CHOPPED

You can buy good quality ready-made tapenade easily in good delis or supermarkets, though it's easy to make your own. Just put some stoned olives in a food processor.

Leek and mushroom flatbreads

Preheat the oven to 220°C/gas mark 7.

Melt the butter in a heavy-based saucepan, add the leeks and mushrooms and gently cook for 3–4 minutes, covered, until the vegetables have softened without colouring. Add the double cream and two-thirds of the Parmesan, season and simmer until the cream has reduced and is just coating the leeks and mushrooms.

Put the flatbread or tortilla onto a baking tray and spread the leek and mushroom mix over, then scatter over the breadcrumbs and the remaining Parmesan. Bake in the oven for about 10–12 minutes until golden, then leave to cool a little. Cut into small squares and serve immediately.

SERVES 6–8

A COUPLE OF GOOD KNOBS OF BUTTER

1 LARGE LEEK, WASHED, HALVED AND CUT INTO ROUGH 1CM DICE

250G OYSTER OR BUTTON MUSHROOMS, SLICED

250ML DOUBLE CREAM

150G FRESHLY GRATED PARMESAN

SALT AND FRESHLY GROUND BLACK PEPPER

A PIECE OF FLATBREAD OR A FLOUR TORTILLA ABOUT 30CM IN DIAMETER

50G FRESH WHITE BREADCRUMBS

Madeleines

Melt the butter and honey in a saucepan over a medium heat and simmer until golden brown. Leave to cool.

In a bowl, whisk the eggs, caster and brown sugar together using an electric beater for 8–10 minutes, until tripled in volume. Fold in the sifted flour and butter mixture until well mixed. Pour into a container and leave to rest for 2–3 hours in the fridge.

Preheat the oven to 180°C/gas mark 4. Grease your madeleine moulds with butter and dust with flour. Place a tablespoon of the mixture in each mould and cook for 12–15 minutes. Leave to cool on a wire rack and store in an airtight container until needed .

MAKES ABOUT 12

135G UNSALTED SOFTENED BUTTER, PLUS EXTRA FOR GREASING

2 TBSP CLEAR HONEY

3 LARGE EGGS

110G CASTER SUGAR

15G SOFT LIGHT BROWN SUGAR

135G SELF-RAISING FLOUR, SIFTED, PLUS EXTRA FOR DUSTING

- - - - - - - - - - - - - - - -

```
These simple little snacky cakes
baked in shell-shaped moulds can
be eaten at any time of the day,
though they are especially good
with tea or as a little after-
dinner nibble.
```

- - - - - - - - - - - - - - - -

Cheese madeleines

Heat the butter in a pan until it foams and begins to colour. Leave to cool. Sieve the flour into a bowl, add 140g of the Cheddar and the salt, then mix in the browned butter and eggs. Pour into a container and leave to rest for 2–3 hours in the fridge.

Preheat the oven to 180°C/gas mark 4. Grease your madeleine moulds and fill with the mixture, scattering the rest of the Cheddar on top. Cook for about 8–10 minutes, until golden. Turn out onto a wire rack to cool and store in an airtight container until required.

MAKES ABOUT 12

135G UNSALTED SOFTENED BUTTER, PLUS EXTRA FOR GREASING

135G SELF-RAISING FLOUR

200G GRATED CHEDDAR

10G SALT

3 LARGE EGGS

- - - - - - - - - - - - - - - -

```
A nice savoury variation of the above
- you could even stick a nugget of
blue cheese in the centre and scatter
a few chopped walnuts on top before
putting them in the oven.
```

- - - - - - - - - - - - - - - -

Savoury choux buns

Put the milk, water, butter, salt and sugar into a saucepan and bring to the boil. Remove from the heat, mix in the flour and Parmesan, if using, and stir with a wooden spoon or spatula until smooth. Return the pan to a low heat and stir for about a minute, until the mixture leaves the sides of the pan. Transfer to a bowl.

Gradually beat the eggs into the mix, one by one, until the pastry is smooth and shiny. Preheat the oven to 180°C/gas mark 4.

Take a non-stick baking tray or line a baking tray with baking parchment. Load the choux pastry into a piping bag and pipe small rounds onto the tray 3–4cm apart. Brush the tops with the egg yolk mixture, scatter over the onion seeds and bake for 10–20 minutes, until the choux buns are golden and crisp. Remove from the oven and leave to cool a little before transferring to a cooling rack.

To make the filling, mix together the cream cheese and chopped chives until well combined. Load the mixture into a piping bag, make a hole in the base of your choux buns and pipe in.

MAKES 40–50 SMALL CHOUX BUNS

125ML MILK

125ML WATER

100G BUTTER, DICED

½ TSP SALT

1 TSP CASTER SUGAR

150G PLAIN FLOUR

60G FINELY GRATED PARMESAN (OPTIONAL)

4 EGGS, BEATEN

1 EGG YOLK MIXED WITH 1 TBSP MILK, TO GLAZE

1 TSP BLACK ONION SEEDS

FOR THE FILLING

150–200G CREAM CHEESE OR FROMAGE FRAIS

1–2 TBSP CHOPPED CHIVES

Choux buns make great little snacks or canapés, piped to the size you wish, and the fillings are just endless. Here I've stuffed them with cream cheese and chives but they are also great filled with smoked salmon trimmings, crème fraîche and chopped dill, or sautéed button or wild mushrooms with finely chopped shallot, cream and grated Parmesan.

BREADS

Fougasse

Put all the ingredients except the olives into a mixer set with the dough hook attachment and mix to a soft dough. Add the olives and knead for 5 minutes on a low speed until smooth and elastic. (You may need to stop the machine occasionally and scrape the sides of the bowl so that everything gets mixed together.) Alternatively, mix by hand until the mixture forms a smooth dough before adding the olives and kneading for 10 minutes. Cover with cling film and leave to prove in a warm place for a few hours until the dough has doubled in volume.

Put the dough on a floured work surface and knead it back to its original size. Divide it into three rough oval shapes. Make 4 slits across each with a knife, cutting right through the dough. Stretch the dough pieces with your hands and a rolling pin to about 30cm long. Put the loaves onto greased baking sheets, cover with cling film or a clean tea towel and leave for about an hour in a warm place to prove until doubled in size. Preheat the oven to 190°C/gas mark 5.

Bake in the oven for 30 minutes until golden. Eat as soon as you can on its own or dipped into a dish of stewed peppers.

MAKES 3 SMALL LOAVES

300G STRONG WHITE BREAD FLOUR, PLUS EXTRA FOR DUSTING

100G WHOLEMEAL FLOUR

1 TSP SALT

1 X 7G SACHET FAST-ACTION YEAST

75ML OLIVE OIL

225ML WARM WATER

4 TBSP CHOPPED BLACK OLIVES

- -

Is fougasse, the famous hearth bread of Provence, poised to become the new focaccia? My local supermarket does one baked with caramelised onions and cheese and I'm always tempted to grab a loaf when I see them in stock, as they tend not to hang around on the shelves too long. It's a simple, rustic bread flat enough to be topped with something like gently cooked sliced onions and cheese, rosemary, baked cloves of garlic or cooked pieces of bacon – whatever you choose.

- -

Wild garlic and cheese bread

Mix the flour, yeast and honey together in a mixer set with the dough hook attachment for 2–3 minutes to make a stiff, elastic dough, adding a little more water during mixing to bring the ingredients together, if necessary. Cover the bowl with cling film and leave to prove in a warm place for a few hours until the dough has doubled in volume.

Meanwhile, heat the remaining oil in a frying pan, add the wild garlic leaves and salt and cook until wilted but not coloured. You may need to do this in batches. Leave to cool.

Remove the dough from the bowl and knead it back to its original size on a lightly floured table, incorporating 4 tablespoons of the olive oil as you go.

Divide the dough in half for two small loaves or leave whole for one large loaf – it's up to you. Shape your dough into one or two rough rectangles and scatter over the wild garlic and three quarters of the cheese. Roll the dough up tightly widthways and transfer, seam-side down, to a lightly oiled baking tray. Cover with a damp tea towel and leave to prove until doubled in size.

Preheat the oven to 240°C/gas mark 8.

Score the top of your bread a few times then dust lightly with flour. Scatter the remaining cheese down the centre. Bake in the oven for 15 minutes. Turn the oven down to 200°C/gas mark 6 and bake for a further 15–20 minutes. Remove from the oven and leave to cool.

MAKES 1 LARGE OR 2 SMALL LOAVES

500G STRONG WHITE BREAD FLOUR, PLUS EXTRA FOR DUSTING

1 X 7G SACHET FAST-ACTION YEAST MIXED WITH ABOUT 150ML WARM WATER

1 TBSP CLEAR HONEY

5 TBSP OLIVE OIL

200G WILD GARLIC LEAVES OR GARLIC CHIVES

2 TSP SALT

150–200G GRATED MATURE CHEDDAR

Wild garlic is a wonderful vegetable to forage for, though you might get stuck on what to do with a large harvest. The combination here of cheese and mellow-flavoured wild garlic is great, with the bread making a perfect snack or accompaniment to a meal. If you haven't got access to wild garlic then garlic chives will do the job.

Farinata

Put the water, salt and chickpea flour into a bowl with the olive oil and stir with a whisk to form a thick batter. Let the mixture stand at room temperature in a warmish place for at least 4–5 hours or, better still, overnight. (This will allow the mixture to start fermenting which gives it its light, airy texture.)

Preheat the oven to 220°C/gas mark 7.

Heat a large, heavy oven-proof frying pan on the stove until it's almost smoking. Cover the bottom generously with olive oil and pour in the mixture to a depth of no more than 6mm, turning the pan as you pour it to coat the bottom evenly. The mixture will begin to bubble. Transfer the pan to the oven and cook for 10–12 minutes until the farinata has set and the edges are crispy. Remove from the pan, and repeat with the rest of the mixture. Serve warm, either on its own as a snack, or with some mixed antipasti or cheese.

SERVES 6–8

1 LITRE WATER

2 TSP SALT

300G CHICKPEA FLOUR, SIFTED

30ML EXTRA VIRGIN OLIVE OIL, PLUS EXTRA FOR FRYING

- -
This is one of the tastiest and simplest things I've eaten for a long time. While it's best cooked in a brick oven to give it that authentic wood-fired flavour, I've had good results with my domestic cooker too. To change it up, try adding a few sliced onions or shallots to the mixture, or scatter over a few rosemary needles or other woody herbs before cooking in the oven.
- -

Pizza bianco

To make the pizza base, mix all of the ingredients together in a mixer set with the dough hook attachment for 2–3 minutes to form a stiff dough, adding a little more water during mixing if the dough isn't coming together. Cover the bowl with cling film and leave to prove in a warm place for a few hours, until the dough has doubled in volume.

Remove the dough from the bowl and knead it back to its original size on a lightly floured table. Using a floured rolling pin, roll the dough out to form two circles roughly 25–30cm in diameter. Transfer the pizza bases to a piece of lightly floured greaseproof paper. Leave the dough to rise a little under a tea towel in a warm place for 30 minutes.

Preheat your oven to its maximum heat and place a circular pizza stone or baking tray inside to heat up for 20 minutes. Take one pizza base, arrange the topping ingredients over it evenly and slide it onto your stone or tray. Bake in the oven for 12–15 minutes, or until the cheese has melted and the crust is golden brown. Repeat for the second pizza.

MAKES 2 PIZZAS

FOR THE BASE

500G STRONG WHITE BREAD FLOUR, PLUS EXTRA FOR DUSTING

1 X 7G SACHET FAST-ACTION YEAST MIXED WITH ABOUT 150ML WARM WATER

1 TBSP CLEAR HONEY

3 TBSP OLIVE OIL

2 TSP SALT

FOR THE TOPPING

1 MEDIUM RED OR WHITE ONION, THINLY SLICED

150G TALEGGIO, SLICED

A HANDFUL OF ROSEMARY NEEDLES

- -

Pizzas are fun to make at home as they are so versatile. You can make the toppings as simple or as sophisticated as you wish. To vary this pizza bianco, try adding a little freshly chopped oregano over it before cooking or even shaving a bit of truffle over the top to make it more luxurious.

- -

Pizza margherita

The stepping stone for all non-white variations on the pizza. Use a reasonable buffalo mozzarella (not the cheap, plastic stuff) and a good-quality passata for the tomato base. From here you can start adding any of your favourite ingredients. Try mixing up the cheeses – scattering over some gorgonzola, say, or other soft Italian cheese.

Wild mushroom pizza

Throw a handful or two of mushrooms into a food processor and whiz to a rough paste. Add to a pan with a little olive oil and butter and cook for a few minutes. Mix in a little grated Parmesan and spread over the pizza bianco base before covering with a few more sliced mushrooms and Taleggio.

Fennel sausage pizza

Skin a couple of traditional Italian fennel sausages and mould the sausagemeat into small meatball-sized pieces using your hands. Add these to either a tomato-based pizza or to a pizza bianco for a delicious, meaty version.

Sourdough

Put all the ingredients except the olive oil into a mixer set with the dough hook attachment and mix together to form a stiff dough, adding a little more water during mixing if the dough isn't coming together. Leave the machine to continue to mix together on a low speed for a few minutes, until your dough is pliable but not sticky. Cover the bowl with cling film, cover with a tea towel and leave in a warm place for 6–7 hours, or overnight, until the dough has risen to twice its volume.

Lightly flour your hands and transfer the dough to a floured work surface. Using your hands, knock the dough back, adding the olive oil to it as you do so. If the dough feels sticky, just knead a little more strong flour into it. Shape the dough into a rough ball.

Dust a wooden bowl or bread proving basket with flour. Lay in the dough, cover with a damp tea towel and leave to rise in a warm place until doubled in size again. Preheat the oven to 240°C/gas mark 8.

Carefully turn the risen dough onto a lightly floured baking tray or pizza stone, keeping the bowl or basket over it, and leave it for another hour in a warm place (in case any of the air has been knocked out while moving it). Remove the bowl or basket, transfer to the oven and bake for 20 minutes. Turn the oven down to 200°C/gas mark 6 and cook for a further 15 minutes, until golden brown.

Transfer to a wire rack and leave to cool to room temperature before slicing.

MAKES 1 LOAF

500G STRONG WHITE BREAD FLOUR, PLUS EXTRA FOR DUSTING

2 TSP SEA SALT

2 TBSP SOURDOUGH STARTER (SEE BELOW)

300–350ML WARM WATER

1 TBSP CLEAR HONEY

1 TBSP NATURAL YOGHURT

2 TBSP OLIVE OIL

- - - - - - - - - - - - - - - - - - - -

The oldest form of bread, sourdough relies on natural air-borne bacteria to cause the bread to rise. Once you've got your own sourdough starter 'activated', a regular feed of water, rye flour and occasionally a little natural sugar in the form of honey will be enough to keep it going. And the more you use it, the better it becomes. The great thing about sourdough is that it lasts for days – try serving it grilled with sliced ripe tomatoes or anchovy fillets drizzled with olive oil. The options are endless.

- - - - - - - - - - - - - - - - - - - -

Sourdough starter Take a clean Kilner jar and mix 3 tablespoons of rye flour with half a tablespoon of honey and 3–4 tablespoons of filtered or spring water to form a thick paste. Leave the jar in a warm place like an airing cupboard for 24 hours with the lid unsealed. Mix in another tablespoon of rye flour and a tablespoon of water, leave for 24 hours again and repeat for a further two days. Now leave the starter out in your kitchen until it begins to naturally ferment. (To speed things along, you could try adding a tablespoon each of natural yoghurt and honey at this stage.) It's at this point that the starter is ready to begin making bread.

Schiacciata con l'uva

Preheat the oven to 230°C/gas mark 8.

Prove your sourdough and knock it back as usual. Using your hands, add two-thirds of the grapes to the dough and knead until mixed together well.

Form the dough into a flattish round about 2cm thick and place on a baking tray. Leave to prove again in a warm place until it has risen to double its size. Gently push the halved figs, if using, into the top of the dough in an even pattern along with the remaining grapes. Bake for 35–45 minutes, until the loaf is golden brown and the fruit are caramelised.

Remove to a wire rack to cool.

MAKES 1 LOAF

1 X SOURDOUGH (SEE PAGE 34), AFTER PROVING AND READY TO SHAPE

500G BLACK GRAPES

4–5 FIGS, HALVED (OPTIONAL)

This is a local sourdough bread traditionally made during the grape harvest in the Chianti region of Tuscany. The grapes are folded into the dough – pips and all – and then the bread is eaten as a snack. I first cooked this bread on holiday and, as we found some great green figs at the market, I thought we'd up the fruit content by adding a few to the dough. There we cooked it in an impressive wood-fired brick oven, but any normal oven will work just as well. You could serve this with cheese or on its own as a tea-time snack, as the locals do.

Spiced cheese cornbread

Preheat the oven to 200°C/gas mark 6.

Heat the oil in a frying pan, add the onion and finely chopped chilli and cook for 5–6 minutes without colouring, stirring every so often. Add the chopped corn kernels and cook, stirring, for another 3–4 minutes. Remove from the heat and leave to cool.

In a bowl, mix the eggs with the cornmeal or polenta, milk, flour, a little salt and pepper and three-quarters of the grated cheese. Beat until well combined before stirring in the cooled onion mixture.

Brush a loaf tin or 22cm round cake tin with olive oil, line the base with a cut-out piece of greaseproof paper and pour in the cornbread mixture. Scatter the sliced chilli over the top and bake for 20 minutes. Remove from the oven and scatter over the remaining cheese before returning to the oven and cooking for a further 10 minutes.

Leave to rest for 10 minutes in the tin before turning out onto a serving dish. Serve warm.

MAKES 1 LOAF

100ML OLIVE OIL, PLUS EXTRA FOR OILING

2 LARGE ONIONS, PEELED, HALVED AND FINELY CHOPPED

4 MEDIUM GREEN CHILLIES, 2 SEEDED AND FINELY CHOPPED AND 2 THINLY SLICED

2 CORN ON THE COB, COOKED AND KERNELS REMOVED OR 400G CANNED SWEETCORN, FINELY CHOPPED

4 LARGE EGGS, BEATEN

200G CORNMEAL OR POLENTA FLOUR

250ML FULL-FAT MILK

200G SELF-RAISING FLOUR

SALT AND FRESHLY GROUND BLACK PEPPER

250G MATURE CHEDDAR, GRATED

- - - - - - - - - - - - - - - -
I often make this unusual bread to take to parties or barbecues and it always gets devoured in no time. It's a great snack with a tomato salsa or as an accompaniment to a brunchy-type soup like a corn chowder.
- - - - - - - - - - - - - - - -

Lahmacun

Mix together the honey and yeast in the water until the yeast has dissolved. Put the flours, olive oil and salt into a mixer set with the dough hook attachment and add the water and yeast mixture. Mix for 2–3 minutes – you may need to stop the machine if it's a large bowl and scrape the sides to make sure all the ingredients are mixed. Alternatively, mix the ingredients together by hand to form a smooth dough before kneading for 5 minutes.

Transfer the dough to a clean bowl, cover with cling film and leave somewhere warm to rise for about an hour, until doubled in size.

Meantime, prepare the topping. Season and fry the lamb and onion in the olive oil on a high heat with the garlic, cinnamon and allspice for 3–4 minutes until lightly coloured, stirring every so often. Add the tomatoes, turn down the heat and cook, stirring occasionally, for a further 3–4 minutes. The mix should be fairly dry; if it's not then leave it on the heat for another minute or so. Add the pine nuts and mint and leave to cool.

Transfer the dough on to a lightly floured surface and, using the heel of your hands, knock the air out of it so it returns to its original size. Divide the mixture into 12 pieces and shape them with your thumb and fingers into little rounds. Preheat the oven to 200°C/gas mark 6. Roll out the pieces into 8–10cm long ovals and put them onto lightly oiled baking trays. Spoon the lamb mixture on thinly in the centre, leaving about a 1cm border around the edges. Cook for 6–7 minutes and eat immediately.

MAKES 12 SMALL FLATBREADS

1 TSP HONEY

3G DRIED YEAST

100ML WARM WATER

100G PLAIN FLOUR

100G WHOLEWHEAT FLOUR

1 TBSP OLIVE OIL

1 TSP SALT

FOR THE TOPPING

SALT AND FRESHLY GROUND BLACK PEPPER

250G MINCED LAMB

1 RED ONION, PEELED AND FINELY CHOPPED

2 TBSP OLIVE OIL

2 GARLIC CLOVES, PEELED AND CRUSHED

⅓ TSP GROUND CINNAMON

⅓ TSP GROUND ALLSPICE

3 TOMATOES, FINELY CHOPPED

2 TBSP PINE NUTS

1 TBSP CHOPPED MINT

- -

Just up the road from where I live in east London there is a Turkish community where you will find flower shops, hairdressers and takeaways open all night. Every so often you come across a shop specialising in lahmacun, the delicious Turkish equivalent of pizza. Thin breads, topped with spicy minced lamb, they're served straight from the oven until they run out – you can't get anything simpler and better to eat.

- -

Blue cheese and chive scones

Preheat the oven to 160°C/gas mark 3.

Sieve the flour, salt and baking powder into a mixing bowl. Rub in the butter until the mix has the texture of breadcrumbs, then slowly mix in just enough cream to form a stiff dough. Roll out the dough on a floured surface to about 2cm thick and cut it out into rounds about 6–7cm across.

Arrange the scones on a baking tray, spacing them evenly apart. Divide the crumbled cheese between them and scatter over the chopped chives.

Bake for 10–15 minutes, until golden. Remove from the oven and serve warm.

MAKES 12 SCONES

225G PLAIN FLOUR

A PINCH OF SALT

2 TSP BAKING POWDER

50G BUTTER, CUT INTO SMALL PIECES

ABOUT 150ML SINGLE CREAM

200–250G BLUE CHEESE, CRUMBLED INTO SMALL PIECES

3 TBSP CHOPPED CHIVES

Scones bring back childhood memories of Dorset cream teas, though these savoury versions — featuring nuggets of blue cheese — make great accompaniments for soups such as onion or watercress. If you don't like blue cheese, try flavouring them with other hard grated cheeses such as Cheddar instead.

FISH & MEAT

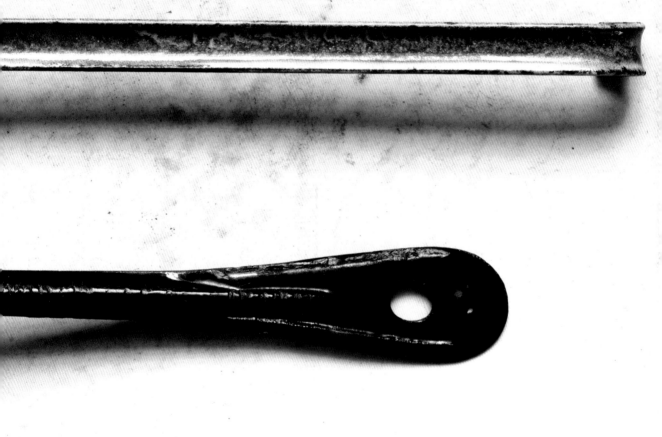

Red mullet en papillote

Preheat the oven to 200°C/gas mark 6. Cut out 4 circles, about 25cm in diameter, of greaseproof or baking paper.

Score the red mullet a few times on one side and lay one, scored-side up, in the centre of each circle of paper. Season the fish, scatter the chillies and spring onions on top and spoon over the olive oil.

Mix the flour with enough water to form a thin paste. Brush or smear the flour paste around the edge of each paper circle. Crimp the edges by folding and rolling the paper over to form a perfect seal all the way around. If it's not sticking then secure the edges with a few paper clips.

Put the paper parcels in the oven and bake for about 12–15 minutes. Serve on plates, opening the paper up at the table and scattering over the coriander to finish.

SERVES 4

4 RED MULLET, ABOUT 180–200G EACH, SCALED, TRIMMED AND GUTTED

SALT AND FRESHLY GROUND BLACK PEPPER

2 MEDIUM RED CHILLIES, TRIMMED, SEEDED AND THINLY SLICED

4 SPRING ONIONS, TRIMMED AND SLICED ON THE ANGLE

2–3 TBSP OLIVE OIL

1 TBSP FLOUR

4–6 TBSP WATER

A FEW SPRIGS OF CORIANDER

Although red mullet has delicate flesh it actually has a robust flavour, which means it can be paired with strong flavours. I've used red chilli and coriander here, but you could add some shredded ginger if you wish. If you have a fish bone phobia, you could always use fillets from a larger fish such as sea bass or grey mullet instead.

Roast lobster with white port and ginger

Preheat the oven to 220°C/gas mark 7.

Place the lobsters in the freezer an hour or so before cooking to make them sleepy (this is deemed to be the most humane way of preparing live lobsters for cooking).

Using a heavy, sharp knife, split the lobsters in half through the head and down the back, pressing down with the palm of your hand to help push the knife through. Crack open the claws and smaller joints to allow heat to get in and ease eating. Make a few scores on the tail meat with the point of the sharp knife. Preheat a grill to its highest setting.

Lay the lobsters on oven trays flesh-side up, and season and brush the flesh with a little olive oil. Roast in the oven for 10 minutes. Alternatively, cook on a hot barbecue for about 5 minutes each side.

Meantime, pour the port into a pan, add the ginger and simmer until reduced by half. Whisk in the butter and parsley.

Transfer the lobsters to warmed serving dishes, pour over the ginger sauce and serve.

SERVES 2

2 LIVE LOBSTERS, ABOUT 500–600G EACH

SALT AND FRESHLY GROUND WHITE PEPPER

1–2 TBSP OLIVE OIL

50–60ML WHITE PORT

30G FRESH ROOT GINGER, PEELED AND FINELY SHREDDED

60–75G CHILLED UNSALTED BUTTER, CUT INTO SMALL PIECES

1 TBSP FINELY CHOPPED FLAT-LEAF PARSLEY

White port is one of those drinks that's almost been forgotten, though I love it with tonic and a slice of lemon. It is also great to cook with, being particularly good with fish and shellfish. The little hint of ginger here gives the dish a delicious kick.

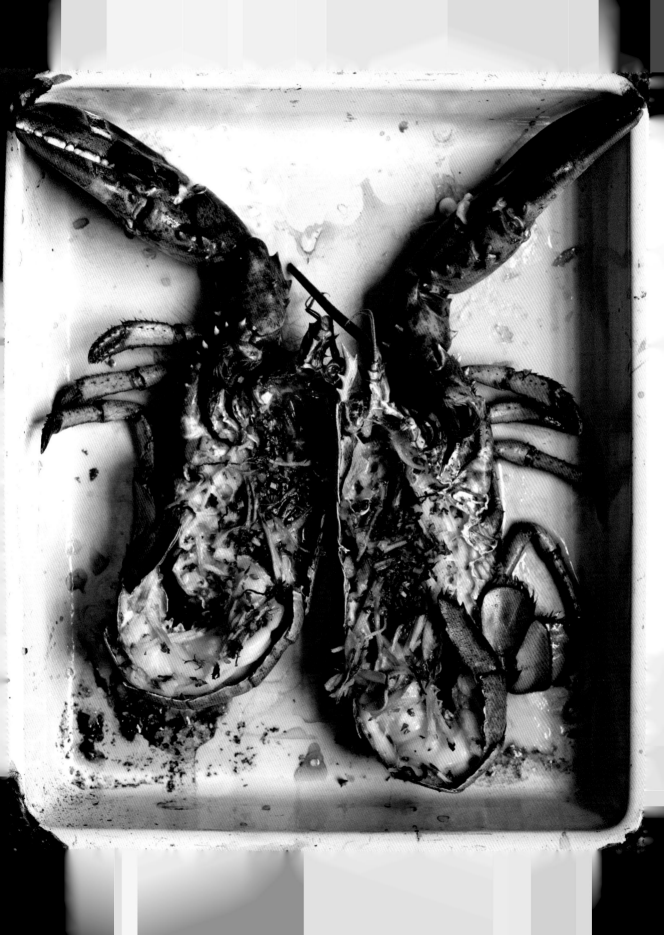

Baked salmon with honey, mustard and dill

Preheat the oven to 240°C/gas mark 8.

Lay the salmon skin-side down on a baking tray or pre-soaked wooden plank. Season the fish then spread with the mustard and scatter the dill or fennel tops over evenly.

Spoon over the honey and bake in the oven for 10–15 minutes, until just cooked. Serve hot or cold with a warm potato salad with sliced shallots and olive oil, or a raw shaved fennel salad.

SERVES 4–6

1 X 1KG SALMON SIDE (WITH SKIN), TRIMMED AND BONES REMOVED

SEA SALT AND FRESHLY GROUND BLACK PEPPER

2 TBSP DIJON OR TEWKESBURY MUSTARD

4–5 TBSP FINELY CHOPPED DILL OR FENNEL TOPS

3–4 TBSP CLEAR HONEY

- -

I found the recipe for this excellent buffet or sharing dish - rather like a hot baked gravadlax without the curing process - in a Russian cookbook. A few years ago I was given a wooden plank by a Scandinavian friend specifically for roasting meat and fish. You pre-soak the plank in water overnight and cook your fish on top of it to impart a slightly smokey flavour, which works perfectly here.

- -

Fish with baker's potatoes

Preheat the oven to 190°C/gas mark 5.

In an oven-proof serving dish large enough to fit the fish, lay the potato and fennel slices in the dish in alternate layers, lightly seasoning every other layer and finishing with a neatly arranged layer of overlapping potatoes. Pour over enough fish stock to cover the vegetables and cook in the oven for about 1 hour, or until the potatoes and fennel are tender and almost cooked through.

Using a sharp knife, score the fish a few times through the skin and lay it gently on top of the potatoes and fennel. Scatter over the rosemary needles, season with salt and pepper, spoon over the olive oil and bake for about 25–30 minutes, until the fish is cooked through but still nice and moist.

SERVES 4-6

2 LARGE BAKING POTATOES, PEELED AND THINLY SLICED

2 FENNEL BULBS, CLEANED AND THINLY SLICED

SEA SALT AND FRESHLY GROUND BLACK PEPPER

500–600ML FISH STOCK

1 X 1.5–2KG WHOLE WHITE FISH, SCALED, TRIMMED AND GUTTED

A HANDFUL OF ROSEMARY NEEDLES

2–3 TBSP OLIVE OIL

This is a great way to cook firm-fleshed fish like bass, sea bream or snapper. The juices from the fish run into the potatoes as it's cooking and the whole dish can go straight from oven to table.

Salt-baked sea bass

An hour before you want to cook the fish, add the water to the salt and mix well in a bowl. Set aside. Spread an additional thin layer of salt on a baking tray or oven-proof serving dish.

Preheat the oven to 250°C/gas mark 9.

Fill the stomach of the fish with the dill or fennel and season with pepper. Lay the bass on the tray and pack the wet salt, about 1cm thick, all over the fish, firming it with your hands. Bake in the oven for 45 minutes.

Have some warm plates ready and a large, clean plate for the bits. Crack the salt a couple of times with the back of a heavy knife then carefully scrape it away from the fish, ensuring you remove as much as possible. (You can do this in front of your guests if you are feeling confident or hide in the kitchen instead – perhaps after showing them the whole thing as it comes out of the oven.)

Remove the head and tail and cut the fish through the body into even-sized portions, giving the underside a final check for salt deposits before transferring it to warm plates. Serve drizzled with some olive oil or melted butter with chopped dill or fennel. Simply cooked green vegetables or a salad are the ideal accompaniments.

SERVES 4–6

1 X 2.5KG SEA BASS, SCALED, GUTTED AND LEFT WHOLE OR BONED (SEE RECIPE INTRO PAGE 56)

240ML WATER

1KG COARSE SEA SALT, PLUS EXTRA FOR LAYERING

4–5 TBSP CHOPPED DILL OR FENNEL TOPS, PLUS EXTRA TO SERVE

FRESHLY GROUND BLACK PEPPER

A LITTLE OLIVE OIL OR MELTED BUTTER TO SERVE

- -

This is a simple, delicious and unusual way to cook firm-textured fish like bass, sea bream or snapper. It seals and cooks the fish without any juices or flavours escaping and makes an impressive dish to show off to your dinner party guests.

- -

Roasted sea bream with oyster stuffing and fennel hollandaise

Preheat the oven to 240°C/gas mark 8. Gently cook the onions in the butter for 4–5 minutes until soft, but not coloured. Transfer them to a bowl, mix with the breadcrumbs, parsley, dill, oysters and juices and season to taste.

Open the sea bream flat onto a table and spread the stuffing mixture evenly down the middle of one fillet. Fold the other fillet over and shape it so the fish looks whole. Score the skin at 3cm intervals along the top, season with salt and pepper and rub with oil. Transfer to an oiled baking tray and roast in the oven for 45 minutes, basting with oil a few times during cooking.

Meantime, make the hollandaise. Melt 15g of the butter in a thick-bottomed saucepan, add the fennel, season and gently cook with a lid on for about 10 minutes, until soft. Remove from the heat and leave to cool. At the same time, place the white wine vinegar, water, shallot, herbs and peppercorns in a saucepan. Bring to the boil and cook for a few minutes until the liquid has reduced to around a dessertspoonful in volume. Sieve and leave to cool.

Melt the remaining butter in a pan and simmer gently for 5 minutes. Remove from the heat, leave to cool a little, then pour off the clarified butter where it has separated from the whey. Put the egg yolks into a bowl with half the vinegar reduction and whisk over a pan of gently simmering water until the mixture begins to thicken and become frothy. Slowly trickle in the clarified butter, whisking continuously. Taste, then add enough of the remaining vinegar reduction to cut through the oiliness of the butter. Season, cover with cling film and leave in a warm place until needed.

Remove the fish from the oven and arrange on a serving platter. Fold the cooked fennel and whipped cream into the hollandaise and serve with the fish and some simply cooked green vegetables.

- -

Oyster stuffing is an American idea - they
use it to stuff turkey for Thanksgiving while
in New Orleans they enjoy it all year round
with a variety of birds. Ask your fishmonger
to bone the bream from the belly, leaving it
attached at the backbone so it ends up
looking a bit like a kipper. The head can be
left on or removed depending on how squeamish
your guests are.

- -

SERVES 6

1 X 2–2.5KG SEA BREAM, SCALED, GUTTED AND BONED

SALT AND FRESHLY GROUND WHITE PEPPER

OLIVE OIL, FOR BRUSHING

FOR THE STUFFING

2 MEDIUM ONIONS, PEELED AND FINELY CHOPPED

100G BUTTER

200G FRESH WHITE BREADCRUMBS

2 TBSP CHOPPED PARSLEY

2 TBSP CHOPPED DILL

10 LARGE OYSTERS, OPENED (SEE PAGE 112) AND CHOPPED WITH THE JUICES RESERVED

FOR THE FENNEL HOLLANDAISE

215G UNSALTED BUTTER

1 FENNEL BULB, FINELY CHOPPED

40ML WHITE WINE VINEGAR

40ML WATER

1 SMALL SHALLOT, PEELED AND CHOPPED

A FEW SPRIGS OF TARRAGON

1 BAY LEAF

5 PEPPERCORNS

3 SMALL EGG YOLKS

100ML DOUBLE CREAM, WHIPPED

Baked baccalau

Place the soaked, well rinsed salt cod in a saucepan with the potatoes, garlic, bay leaf and cayenne pepper. Cover with the milk, bring to the boil and simmer for 8–10 minutes, or until the potatoes are well cooked. Remove the cod and potatoes with a slotted spoon and set to one side. Preheat the oven to 200°C/gas mark 6.

Put the potato and half the cod into a food processer and blend coarsely with enough of the hot milk to make a sloppy purée. Flake the rest of the cod into the mix, season to taste and stir in the cream. Transfer to a large oven-proof dish or individual serving dishes.

Mix the breadcrumbs, cheese and butter together in a bowl. Scatter the breadcrumb mixture over the fish mixture and bake in the oven for about 20–25 minutes, until nicely browned and hot in the middle. Serve immediately.

SERVES 4

250G BONELESS SALT COD, SOAKED OVERNIGHT AND RINSED THOROUGHLY SEVERAL TIMES

250G POTATOES, PEELED AND SLICED

6 GARLIC CLOVES, PEELED AND SLICED

½ BAY LEAF

A PINCH OF CAYENNE PEPPER

200–300ML MILK

100ML DOUBLE CREAM

40G FRESH WHITE BREADCRUMBS

30G FINELY GRATED MATURE CHEDDAR OR PARMESAN

30G BUTTER, MELTED

- - - - - - - - - - - - - - - - -

This is an easy to serve all-year-round starter, rather like fish pie, which can also be served as a main with salad. Try to buy the good-quality salt cod pieces that are normally sold in good Spanish or Portuguese delis rather than the big West Indian stuff that resembles cricket bats and needs days of soaking.

- - - - - - - - - - - - - - - - -

Chicken baked in the pot with garlic

Preheat the oven to 240°C/gas mark 8.

Season the chicken inside and out, halve the garlic horizontally and place in a clay pot or casserole dish with the bird. Rub the breasts with the butter.

Place the chicken in the oven and cook, uncovered, for 20 minutes. Turn the oven down to 190°C/gas mark 5. Scatter the rosemary over the chicken, baste it with some of the juices, cover with the lid and cook for a further 40–50 minutes.

To serve, simply place the pot on the table and let guests carve and help themselves, or remove the chicken from the pot and cut and joint it in the kitchen, before returning to the pot to serve.

SERVES 4

1 X 1.5–2KG GOOD-QUALITY CHICKEN

SALT AND FRESHLY GROUND BLACK PEPPER

1 BULB OF JUMBO GARLIC, OR 2–3 NORMAL SIZED BULBS

A COUPLE OF GOOD KNOBS OF BUTTER

A FEW SPRIGS OF ROSEMARY

Clay pots are great for cooking meat. Traditionally this method of cooking is referred to as a pot roast, with the tight-fitting lid retaining all the juices in the pot — creating a steam which helps keep your meat nice and moist. A good-quality chicken here is crucial to the end result, and generally the more you pay for your bird, the better it will be. Here I've used a bulb of the sweet, large jumbo or elephant garlic, though normal garlic bulbs work just fine.

Honey-baked ham

Preheat the oven to 160°C/gas mark 3.

Score the skin or fat of the ham joint with a knife in a criss-cross pattern about 5mm deep, then stud the cloves in randomly. Line a roasting tray with two or three layers of foil and place the ham on top. Scatter over the brown sugar and pepper.

Place the ham in the oven and bake for half an hour. Spoon over a quarter of the honey and continue to cook, basting regularly and adding a further quarter of the honey every half an hour, for a further 2 hours. Turn up the oven up to 200°C/gas mark 6 for about 20–30 minutes so the ham is nicely glazed. If the basting juices begin to burn during cooking, just add a little water to the tray.

Remove from the oven and transfer the ham to a fresh dish and continue coating it with any excess cooking juices while it's cooling. Serve the ham at room temperature or cold.

SERVES 8–10

1 X 2KG BONED AND ROLLED UNCOOKED HAM OR GAMMON, WITH OR WITHOUT THE RIND

12 CLOVES

80G BROWN SUGAR

½ TBSP COARSELY GROUND BLACK PEPPER

150–200G CLEAR HONEY

A home-made baked ham or gammon is a great thing to have around during festive periods to serve as a main course, or as part of a buffet. I also love it for breakfast with a fried duck's egg and mustard. If you're using a tender joint I would suggest baking it directly following the method above. If, however, you are using a secondary cut like a shoulder joint or a hock then try boiling it until tender first then finishing it as above.

Pheasant biryani

Mix the pheasant thighs together with the ginger, garlic, garam masala, chilli powder, turmeric, chillies, cumin, curry leaves, cardamom and coriander in a stainless-steel or non-reactive bowl. Cover with cling film and leave to marinate in the fridge for 3–4 hours.

Rinse the rice a couple of times in cold water to remove excess starch, then drain in a sieve. Heat the ghee in a large heavy-based frying pan over a medium-high heat, add the onions and fry for about 10 minutes, stirring, until golden brown. Drain in a sieve over a bowl to reserve the ghee.

Remove the pheasant from the marinade (reserving it for later). Return three-quarters of the ghee to the pan, add the pheasant a few pieces at a time and fry, turning, until lightly browned on all sides. Transfer to an oven-proof serving dish with a lid, add the yoghurt, browned onions and remaining marinade and cook on a low heat for 40–50 minutes, until the pheasant is tender. Remove from the heat.

Cook the rice in plenty of boiling salted water for 5 minutes, drain well, then spread over the meat. Spoon over the remaining ghee and the saffron-infused milk. Preheat the oven to 220°C/gas mark 7.

Mix the flour and salt with enough water to form a smooth, elastic dough. Roll the dough with your hands into a sausage shape long enough to fit around the cooking dish. Press the dough around the dish edge and press the lid lightly onto the dough. Put the pot over a high heat for a few minutes to bring the contents to the boil before transferring to the oven for 40 minutes. Break the dough seal to serve.

SERVES 4–6

12 PHEASANT THIGHS, BONED AND SKINNED

60G FRESH ROOT GINGER, PEELED AND FINELY GRATED

4 GARLIC CLOVES, PEELED AND CRUSHED

2 TBSP GARAM MASALA

½ TSP CHILLI POWDER

½ TSP GROUND TURMERIC

4 SMALL GREEN, MEDIUM-HEAT CHILLIES, FINELY CHOPPED

1 TSP GROUND CUMIN

A GOOD PINCH OF CURRY LEAVES

12–15 GREEN CARDAMOM PODS, SEEDS REMOVED AND CRUSHED

2 TBSP CHOPPED CORIANDER LEAVES

500G BASMATI RICE

200G GHEE OR BUTTER

4 LARGE ONIONS, PEELED AND THINLY SLICED

250ML THICK NATURAL YOGHURT

A GOOD PINCH OF SAFFRON STRANDS, SOAKED IN 2 TBSP HOT MILK

FOR THE SEALING DOUGH

150G WHOLEWHEAT FLOUR

1 TSP SALT

100–120ML WATER

This is not the kind of biryani you'll find in your average curry house, which is unfortunate because a well-made biryani has a lot going for it. This makes an impressive dinner party dish if you are putting on an Indian spread – lift the lid off at the table to reveal the fluffy rice and saffron and the fragrant spices underneath. I've noticed pheasant thighs becoming more readily available in supermarkets and good butchers, but if you are struggling to find them you could always use chicken thighs, lamb, mutton or even venison instead.

Slow-cooked stuffed breast of mutton with wild garlic and fennel

Preheat the oven to 220°C/gas mark 7. To make the stuffing, gently cook the onion in the butter for a couple of minutes until soft. Transfer to a bowl and leave to cool a little. Roughly chop the wild garlic and add to the bowl with the mince and offal, if using. Season and mix together well.

Lay the mutton breast skin-side down on a work surface or board and spoon the stuffing down the centre. Roll up tightly and tie with string at 2–3cm intervals. Season.

Heat a roasting tray in the oven for 10 minutes. Remove the hot tray from the oven, add the mutton and roast for 25–30 minutes, turning every so often. Lower the setting to 160°C/gas mark 3. Remove the mutton from the tray and scatter the sliced fennel and onion down its centre, repositioning the mutton on top. Return to the oven to cook for a further 1 ½–2 hours, basting every so often. If the onion and fennel slices look as if they are browning too much, cover the mutton with foil. Once cooked, remove the mutton, cover in foil and set aside for about 10 minutes to rest.

While the meat is resting, transfer the roasted fennel and onion to a saucepan with the cooking juices and water and leave to simmer for 3–4 minutes. Chop the wild garlic and add to the sauce. Transfer half the sauce to a food processor and coarsely blend, before returning to the pan and leaving to simmer for a further 2–3 minutes. To serve, remove the string from the mutton and slice into 1–2cm slices. Arrange on plates and pour over the sauce to finish.

SERVES 4

1 X 500G MUTTON OR LAMB BREAST, BONED

1 FENNEL BULB, HALVED AND FINELY SLICED

1 ONION, PEELED, HALVED AND FINELY SLICED

3 TBSP FRESH WHITE BREADCRUMBS

3–4 TBSP WATER

2 HANDFULS OF WILD GARLIC LEAVES, WASHED AND DRIED

FOR THE STUFFING

1 SMALL ONION, PEELED, HALVED AND FINELY CHOPPED

A GOOD KNOB OF BUTTER

A HANDFUL OF WILD GARLIC LEAVES, WASHED AND DRIED

200G COARSE MUTTON OR LAMB MINCE AND/OR A MIX OF SWEETBREADS, LIVER, HEART AND KIDNEYS

SALT AND FRESHLY GROUND BLACK PEPPER

Breast of mutton is one of the most under-used cuts of meat. Its fattiness puts people off, but stuffed and slowly cooked it makes for a tasty, cheap meal. The breast can be stuffed with any of the lesser cuts such as minced shin or neck, or with offal as I suggest here. Fennel may not seem like an obvious partner for lamb but its subtle, aniseed flavour works a treat.

Veal baked in hay

Preheat the oven to 220°C/gas mark 7.

Season the veal with salt and pepper. Heat a little vegetable oil until almost smoking in a large, heavy frying pan, add the meat and seal on all sides until nicely browned. Remove from the pan.

Using a sharp knife, make about 10 incisions about 1cm deep through the skin of the veal and insert a slice of garlic and a sprig of rosemary into each. Put the veal into a roasting tray and pack the hay around it. Cover with foil and cook in the oven for 35 minutes. Remove the foil and turn the oven down to 190°C/gas mark 5 and cook for another 15 minutes.

To serve, leave to rest for 15 minutes, remove the hay and carve. (This will give you meat cooked to medium-rare – if you leave the veal to rest in the hay for a further 15–20 minutes it will continue cooking to medium.)

SERVES 4

1 X 1.5KG RIB OR RACK OF VEAL

SALT AND FRESHLY GROUND BLACK PEPPER

A LITTLE VEGETABLE OIL, FOR FRYING

1 NEW-SEASON GARLIC BULB OR A FEW NORMAL GARLIC CLOVES, PEELED AND THINLY SLICED

10 SMALL SPRIGS OF ROSEMARY

A COUPLE OF GOOD HANDFULS OF CLEAN HAY, SOAKED IN COLD WATER FOR 15 MINUTES AND DRAINED

- - - - - - - - - - - - - - - - -
Cooking with hay is an old technique
– the hay keeps the heat in and gives
the meat a fantastic grassy taste. It's
important to soak the hay before using
though, because if it smoulders it will
give the delicate veal a flavour you
don't want. Pet shops and garden
centres sell clean hay.
- - - - - - - - - - - - - - - - -

Venison and parsnip hotpot

Preheat the oven to 220°C/gas mark 7.

Season the venison chunks with salt and pepper and dust with flour. Heat a heavy-bottomed frying pan with half of the vegetable oil, add the venison a few pieces at a time and fry until nicely coloured, then remove to a colander to drain.

Clean the pan, add the remaining vegetable oil and heat. Add the onions and fry over a high heat until they begin to colour, then add the butter and continue to cook for a few minutes until the onions soften. Dust the onions with a tablespoon of flour, stir well, then gradually add the beef stock, stirring to avoid lumps. Scatter over the rosemary, bring to the boil, season with salt and pepper and simmer for about 10 minutes.

To assemble the hotpot, cover the bottom of a deep oven-proof casserole dish with a layer of potatoes and parsnips. Follow this with a layer of meat moistened with a little sauce, then add another layer of potatoes and parsnips. Continue in this way until the meat and most of the sauce has been used, finishing with a final layer of overlapping potato and parsnip slices. Brush the top with a little of the sauce.

Cover the casserole with a lid and cook in the oven for about 30 minutes. Turn the oven down to 140°C/gas mark 1 and cook slowly for a further 2 hours, or until the meat is tender.

Remove the lid and turn the oven back up to 220°C/gas mark 7. Brush the potato topping with a little melted butter and return to the oven for 15 minutes or so to allow the potatoes to brown. Serve with pickled red cabbage (as they do up North), seasonal root vegetables or greens.

SERVES 4–6

1 X 800–1KG VENISON PIECE (NECK, INNER HAUNCH MUSCLE ETC.), CUT INTO ROUGH 3–4CM CHUNKS

SALT AND PEPPER

PLAIN FLOUR, FOR DUSTING

4 TBSP VEGETABLE OIL

450–500G ONIONS, PEELED AND THINLY SLICED

60G UNSALTED BUTTER, PLUS EXTRA, MELTED, FOR BRUSHING

800ML BEEF STOCK

½ TSP CHOPPED ROSEMARY LEAVES

500G LARGE POTATOES, PEELED AND THINLY SLICED

500G PARSNIPS, PEELED AND THINLY SLICED

- -

Hotpots need not be made with lamb or mutton only - game meats like deer, wild boar or even rabbit all make for great-flavoured, hearty versions. Venison is a generic term, covering different species of deer including the roe deer, red deer, fallow and muntjac, all of which vary in size and have different eating qualities. Butchers often tend to mix up venison cuts, which can result in you having a pot full of pieces of meat with lots of different cooking times. Ask for meat that comes from a single cut to make sure this isn't the case.

- -

Meatloaf

Preheat the oven to 190°C/gas mark 5.

Heat 1 tablespoon of the vegetable oil in a pan, add the onion, garlic and thyme and cook gently for a few minutes until the onion is soft. Transfer to a bowl and leave to cool.

Add the minced pork, beef and breadcrumbs to the cooled onion mixture and mix well. Add the Worcestershire sauce, Dijon mustard and celery salt and season. Test the mixture by taking a little of it, shaping it into a flat cake and gently pan-frying it. Taste and add more seasoning or Worcestershire sauce if needed. Press the mixture into a 900g loaf tin or a large terrine mould and cover the top with kitchen foil.

Fill a deep roasting tin with hot water to a depth of 4cm (this will act as a bain-marie, or water bath, for your meatloaf). Gently place the meatloaf in the middle of the tin and transfer carefully to the middle shelf of the oven. Cook for 50 minutes to 1 hour, testing the meatloaf by inserting a thin knife or roasting fork in the centre – if it's hot in the middle, it's cooked.

Remove the meatloaf from the bain-marie and leave to cool. Once cool, place in the refrigerator for a few hours to set.

To serve, remove the meatloaf from the tin and cut into 1½–2cm slices. Heat the remaining oil in a large frying pan, add the slices in batches and cook for a couple of minutes on each side until golden. Keep the cooked slices warm in a low oven until ready to serve.

SERVES 6–8

3 TBSP VEGETABLE OIL

2 ONIONS, PEELED, HALVED AND FINELY CHOPPED

2 GARLIC CLOVES, PEELED AND CRUSHED

2 TSP THYME LEAVES

300G COARSELY MINCED FATTY PORK

300G COARSELY MINCED BEEF OR VEAL

150G FRESH WHITE BREADCRUMBS

2 TBSP WORCESTERSHIRE SAUCE

2 TSP DIJON MUSTARD

1 TSP CELERY SALT

SALT AND FRESHLY GROUND BLACK PEPPER

A meatloaf makes a perfect breakfast, brunch or lunch dish. You can jazz it up a bit by sticking a fried egg and wild mushrooms over it or just serve it with some mashed potato or chips. It's also great for snacking on like a pâté as a part of a picnic. You can substitute the pork with veal if you wish as long as it's got some fat in it to keep it moist.

Tamarind-baked back ribs

Smear the ribs with the marinade ingredients in a stainless-steel or non-reactive bowl. Cover with cling film and leave to marinate in the fridge for at least 24 hours (the longer the better).

Preheat the oven to 190°C/gas mark 5. Transfer the marinated ribs to a baking or roasting tin and cook for 30 minutes, basting as they are cooking. Turn the oven down to 160°C/gas mark 3, cover the tray with foil and continue cooking and basting for another hour, then remove the foil and cook, basting, for a further 30–45 minutes. Remove the ribs from the oven and serve whole or cut into sections with a simple green salad, coleslaw or baked sweet potatoes (see page 87).

SERVES 4–6

1–2 PORK BACK RIB RACKS, ABOUT 1.5–2KG

FOR THE MARINADE

100G TAMARIND PASTE

100G POMEGRANATE MOLASSES

6 GARLIC CLOVES, PEELED AND CRUSHED

60G ROOT GINGER, PEELED AND GRATED

½ TBSP GROUND CUMIN

- - - - - - - - - - - -

Rib racks can be found in most butchers (I've even seen them in supermarkets) while you might need to head to an Asian or middle eastern shop or good deli to get hold of tamarind paste and pomegranate molasses. You can use beef ribs here if you like, though bear in mind they will need a bit more cooking.

- - - - - - - - - - - -

VEGETABLES

Armenian tomato and aubergine salad

Preheat the oven to its hottest setting. Place the aubergines on a baking tray, transfer to the oven and bake for 40–50 minutes, turning every so often, until the skins are blackened and burnt. Remove from the oven and leave to cool.

Cut the cooled aubergines in half and scoop out the flesh as close to the skin as you can (this will give you a really good, smoky flavour). Chop the flesh over several times until it's almost a purée, then transfer to a bowl with the garlic, chilli, tomatoes, spring onions, olive oil and coriander. Season and mix together well.

Scatter over a few extra coriander leaves and serve at room temperature with some warm flatbread or farinata (see page 30).

SERVES 4–6

3 MEDIUM AUBERGINES

2 GARLIC CLOVES, PREFERABLY NEW-SEASON, PEELED AND CRUSHED

1 RED CHILLI, HALVED, SEEDED AND FINELY CHOPPED

350–400G RIPE TOMATOES, FINELY CHOPPED

4 SPRING ONIONS, FINELY CHOPPED

150ML EXTRA VIRGIN OLIVE OIL

2–3 TBSP CHOPPED CORIANDER LEAVES, PLUS EXTRA TO SERVE

This is rather like one of those salads that you find in Turkish restaurants, and it's a great dish to put on the table as a sharing starter. You can make this as fine or as coarse as you like – I prefer chopping the ingredients by hand, but you could also give all the ingredients a whiz in a food processor if you wish.

Escalivada

Fire up your wood-fired oven or set your conventional oven to its highest setting. Line two baking trays with kitchen foil and arrange the peppers and aubergines on one and the onions on the other. Brush the pepper and aubergine skins with a little vegetable oil, place in the oven along with the onions and cook for 30–45 minutes, until the skins begin to blacken and blister and the peppers and aubergines soften. You may need to leave the onions in a little longer, depending on their size.

Put the peppers in a bowl, cover with cling film and leave to cool a little (the steam this creates enables the skins to be removed more easily). Leave the onions and aubergines to cool on the trays.

Remove the cooled peppers from the bowl and cut in half lengthways. Using your hands, remove the skins and seeds, cutting away any skin that's proving tricky with a knife. Quarter the aubergines lengthways and cut the flesh away close to the skin with a knife. Halve the onions and remove the skins.

To serve, cut the pepper and aubergine flesh into strips, quarter the onions and arrange on a dish. Whisk the sherry vinegar and olive oil together in a small bowl and season to taste. Spoon the dressing over the vegetables and scatter over the basil or oregano to finish.

SERVES 4–6

4 THICK-FLESHED SWEET GREEN OR RED PEPPERS

4 AUBERGINES

6 RED ONIONS

A LITTLE VEGETABLE OR CORN OIL, FOR BRUSHING

½ TBSP SHERRY VINEGAR

4–6 TBSP EXTRA VIRGIN OLIVE OIL

SALT AND FRESHLY GROUND BLACK PEPPER

A SMALL HANDFUL OF GREEK BASIL OR OREGANO LEAVES

- -

This dish of roasted vegetables - generally made with sweet green or red peppers, aubergines and onions - is commonly found in the Catalan region of Spain. It translates as 'cooked in the embers', and is the perfect dish to cook in a wood-fired oven once you have finished cooking other dishes, though it can be cooked in a conventional oven set to its hottest temperature, under a very hot grill or on a covered barbecue as well.

- -

Tomato freekeh

Preheat the oven to 180°C/gas mark 4. Cut the tomatoes into roughly 1 centimetre dice. Set aside. Rinse and drain the freekeh.

Melt 60g of the butter in an oven-proof dish, add the onion and garlic and cook gently for 2–3 minutes, until soft. Stir in the drained freekeh, add the stock mixture and season to taste. Bake in the oven for 40 minutes or until the freekeh is tender, adding a little more stock if it looks as though it is drying out. Stir in the tomatoes and the remaining butter and cook for a few more minutes, until the freekeh is risotto-like in consistency – you may need to add a little more stock. Check and adjust the seasoning, if necessary, and serve.

SERVES 4

4 TOMATOES

150G FREEKEH, SOAKED IN WATER FOR 2 HOURS

100G BUTTER

1 MEDIUM ONION, PEELED, HALVED AND FINELY CHOPPED

4 GARLIC CLOVES, PEELED AND CRUSHED

600–700ML HOT VEGETABLE STOCK, MIXED WITH 3 TBSP TOMATO PURÉE

SALT AND FRESHLY GROUND BLACK PEPPER

- -

This is rather like a rice pilaf but made with freekeh, a lightly roasted green wheat that is often used in Arabic and Egyptian cooking. It is delicious served either hot or warm as a colourful garnish for fish or meat, while topped with pieces of fried haloumi it makes a great vegetarian alternative.

- -

Lobster thermidor baked potatoes

Preheat the oven to 200°C/gas mark 6.

Wash the potatoes, transfer to the oven and bake them for about 1–1½ hours, or until soft. Leave them to cool a little, then cut off about a quarter of the top of each potato and scoop the flesh out into a bowl. Mash as chunky or as smooth as you wish, then mix with the butter and season to taste. Return the potato skins to the oven for about 10 minutes to crisp up before setting aside with the flesh.

Meantime, simmer the white wine with the shallot until the liquid has almost evaporated. Add the mustard and fish stock and reduce again similarly. Add the cream, reserving a tablespoon, bring back to the boil and simmer until the sauce has reduced by half or more and is quite thick. Add the Parmesan and 60g of the grated Cheddar and whisk until smooth. Season and leave to cool. (You can add a little more mustard at this stage to taste if you want the sauce a little more tangy.)

In a small bowl, whip the remaining tablespoon of double cream until it forms soft peaks. Fold into the cooled sauce with the egg yolk.

Turn up the oven to 240°C/gas mark 8. Halve the body of the lobster lengthways and remove the meat from the shell. Cut the tail meat into four or five pieces. Crack the claws and leg joints and remove all of the meat. Remove the claws from each lobster, then crack and remove all of the meat, including the smaller joints.

Mix half of the sauce with the mashed potato and spoon into the crisp potato shells, leaving about a centimetre from the top of each. Arrange the lobster on top of the potato, scatter over the remaining cheese and spoon over the rest of the sauce. Return to the oven or place under a hot grill until nicely browned. Serve with a few dressed salad leaves.

SERVES 4

4 BAKING POTATOES

80G BUTTER

SALT AND FRESHLY GROUND BLACK PEPPER

50ML WHITE WINE

1 LARGE SHALLOT, PEELED AND FINELY CHOPPED

2 TSP ENGLISH MUSTARD

100ML FISH STOCK (OR A THIRD OF A GOOD-QUALITY STOCK CUBE DISSOLVED IN 100ML HOT WATER)

300ML DOUBLE CREAM

30G PARMESAN, GRATED

80G MATURE CHEDDAR, GRATED

1 SMALL EGG YOLK

1 X 500–600G COOKED LOBSTER

This is a great way to stretch out a lobster and makes for a fantastic, luxurious baked potato. Extravagant you may think, but not really. The baked potato is making a bit of a comeback – I'm sure they'll soon be dished up in all the smart restaurants...

Mutton shepherd's pie potatoes

Preheat the oven to 200°C/gas mark 6.

Wash the potatoes and bake in the oven for about 1½ hours until soft. Scoop out the flesh and mash through a potato ricer or by hand as fine as possible, then mix in the butter and enough milk to cream the potatoes. Season to taste. Return the potato skins to the oven for about 10 minutes to crisp up before setting aside with the flesh.

Meantime, prepare the filling. Season the mince and heat half the vegetable oil in a heavy-based frying pan until almost smoking. Add the meat in small quantities and cook for a few minutes, stirring, until browned all over, then drain in a colander to remove any fat.

In a separate thick-bottomed saucepan, heat the remaining vegetable oil and gently cook the onion, celery, garlic and thyme for 2–3 minutes, stirring every so often, until softened. Add the browned meat and flour and mix together well. Add the tomato purée and continue to cook over a low heat, stirring, for a few minutes, before adding the red wine, Worcestershire sauce and stock gradually. Bring to the boil, lower to a simmer and continue to cook for about an hour, until the liquid has thickened and the meat is tender. Remove from the heat, check the seasoning and leave to cool.

Spoon the mutton into the potatoes until about two-thirds full. Now spoon or pipe the mashed potato on top until the potato mix is sitting a few centimetres above the top of the potato skins. Scatter over the breadcrumbs and Cheddar and bake for about 40 minutes, until the topping is golden brown and the filling is hot.

SERVES 4

4 LARGE BAKING POTATOES

40G BUTTER

40–50ML MILK

SALT AND FRESHLY GROUND BLACK PEPPER

500G COARSELY MINCED MUTTON SHOULDER OR NECK

2 TBSP VEGETABLE OIL, FOR FRYING

1 MEDIUM ONION, PEELED, HALVED AND FINELY CHOPPED

1 STICK OF CELERY, CUT INTO ROUGH ½CM DICE

1 GARLIC CLOVE, PEELED AND CRUSHED

A FEW SPRIGS OF THYME, LEAVES REMOVED

½ TBSP PLAIN FLOUR

½ TBSP TOMATO PURÉE

1 GLASS OF RED WINE

½ TBSP WORCESTERSHIRE SAUCE

500ML HOT BEEF STOCK

15G FRESH WHITE BREADCRUMBS

15G MATURE CHEDDAR, GRATED

- - - - - - - - - - - -
Another nice variation on
a baked potato. You can
make the filling here from
scratch or use excess
from a shepherd's pie.
- - - - - - - - - - - -

Patatas Els Tinars

Gently cook the onion, garlic and ham in the olive oil for 2–3 minutes until soft. Add the minced pork, thyme and pimentón, season and cook on a high heat for a couple more minutes, stirring, until the meat is lightly coloured. Add the tomato purée and pour over just enough water to cover the meat. Simmer gently for about 10–15 minutes, or until the liquid has evaporated.

Meantime, preheat the oven to 200°C/gas mark 6.

Arrange the potato slices in a large, oiled tray into 4 roughly-shaped circles measuring about 15cm in diameter – the slices should be overlapping and the circles formed of 2–3 layers. Season lightly before adding a final layer of potatoes to each. Brush the circles with olive oil and bake for about 20 minutes. Spread the pork mixture in a thin layer over each circle and return to the oven for another 20 minutes, until lightly browned (if they look as though they are starting to brown too much, cover with foil and turn the oven down a little). Serve them just as they are.

SERVES 4

1 MEDIUM ONION, PEELED AND FINELY CHOPPED

2 GARLIC CLOVES, PEELED AND CRUSHED

30–40G CURED HAM TRIMMINGS, BACON OR PANCETTA, FINELY CHOPPED

2 TBSP OLIVE OIL, PLUS EXTRA FOR BRUSHING

80G MINCED PORK BELLY

½ TSP CHOPPED THYME LEAVES

A GOOD PINCH OR TWO OF PIMENTON (SPANISH PAPRIKA)

SALT AND FRESHLY GROUND BLACK PEPPER

1 TSP TOMATO PURÉE

2 LARGE BAKING POTATOES, PEELED AND CUT INTO 2–3MM SLICES

I came across this dish years ago in a restaurant called Els Tinars near Sant Feliu on the Costa Brava. The restaurant had a Michelin star, but the food was simple and reflected what grew and was hunted locally. I remember eating trays full of local snails and simply grilled saffron milk cap mushrooms, but the recipe that has stayed with me is this simple potato dish. It must have been conceived as a way of using up some of the trimmings from the cured hams, as the fat is delicious when cooked. It was served as a starter, but I think it would also make a great supper dish.

Pommes Anna

Preheat the oven to 200°C/gas mark 6.

Heat a 26cm cast iron pot or a deep oven-proof non-stick frying pan on top of the stove or in the oven. Remove the pan from the heat and rub the bottom of it with a little of the goose fat.

Lay over enough potato slices to cover the surface of the pan, season lightly and rub with a little more goose fat. Continue to layer the pan with potatoes, lightly seasoning and rubbing with goose fat every couple of layers, until the potatoes are all used up.

Bake in the oven for 1 hour until soft and golden brown, testing that the potatoes are tender with the point of a knife. If the potatoes look as though they are browning early, cover with foil. Turn the potato cake out onto a chopping board and cut into equal wedges to serve.

SERVES 6–8

20G GOOSE OR DUCK FAT

1KG LARGE POTATOES, PEELED AND THINLY SLICED

SALT AND FRESHLY GROUND BLACK PEPPER

- -

One of my favourite cooking equipment finds was in E. Dehillerin, a fantastic shop in Paris that supplies the trade with cooking equipment and utensils. Sitting among all the copper saucepans was a two-piece pot used for baking and serving this classic potato dish. The larger part of the pot is used to hold the potatoes and the smaller lid for turning out and serving. Pommes Anna is rarely found on menus these days, although it still sticks clearly in my mind from college days. It makes a great centre piece on the dinner table, and is an excellent accompaniment to meat dishes.

- -

Baked sweet potatoes with honey and chilli

Preheat the oven to 200°C/gas mark 6.

Score the sweet potato flesh in a criss-cross with the point of a sharp knife, transfer to a baking tray and season with salt and pepper. Divide the butter between the halves, then scatter over the chilli slices and cheese, if using. Spoon the honey over each, cover with foil and bake for 30 minutes. Remove the foil and continue cooking for another 15 minutes or so until the potatoes feel tender to the point of a knife. Serve with grilled or roasted meats or fish.

SERVES 4

4 MEDIUM-SIZED SWEET POTATOES, WASHED AND HALVED

SALT AND FRESHLY GROUND BLACK PEPPER

40G BUTTER

2 SMALL RED OR GREEN CHILLIES, FINELY CHOPPED

80G MATURE CHEDDAR, GRATED (OPTIONAL)

1–2 TBSP CLEAR HONEY

- -

Baked sweet potatoes are great with barbecues or as an accompaniment to a roast. I've found they also satisfy vegetarians as they have that little something that an ordinary baked potato doesn't - especially if you scatter a little extra cheese over the top of them a few minutes before removing them from the oven.

- -

Portuguese baked breakfast eggs

Heat the olive oil in a heavy-based (preferably oven-proof) saucepan over a low heat, add the chorizo, onion and garlic and gently cook for 6–7 minutes without colouring. Add the tomatoes, season with salt and pepper and simmer gently for 30 minutes, stirring every so often.

Preheat the oven to 180°C/gas mark 4. If you are using an oven-proof pan, crack the eggs over the tomatoes, ensuring they are evenly spaced. Alternatively divide the tomato mixture evenly between individual oven-proof dishes, cracking an egg into the centre of each. Bake in the oven for about 8–10 minutes, or until the eggs are just cooked.

Drizzle over a little olive oil and serve immediately.

- - - - - - - - - - - - - - -

I had this dish in Portugal a while back as a starter for dinner, but I think it also makes a great breakfast dish.

- - - - - - - - - - - - - - -

SERVES 4

2 TBSP OLIVE OIL, PLUS EXTRA FOR DRIZZLING

150G COOKING CHORIZO, FINELY CHOPPED

1 MEDIUM ONION, PEELED AND FINELY CHOPPED

4 GARLIC CLOVES, PEELED AND CRUSHED

2 X 400G CANS OF GOOD-QUALITY CHOPPED TOMATOES, OR 1KG SKINNED RIPE TOMATOES

SALT AND FRESHLY GROUND BLACK PEPPER

4 FREE-RANGE EGGS

Baked duck's eggs with wild mushrooms

Preheat the oven to 180°C/gas mark 4. Heat half the butter in a pan, add the mushrooms and cook gently for 3–4 minutes, covered, until softened. Add the cream, season with salt and pepper and simmer very gently for 3–4 minutes. Stir in the parsley and continue to simmer for another minute. The sauce should remain quite thin – if it does look as though it has thickened, add a little water.

Meantime, grease four individual ramekins or shallow oven-proof serving dishes with the remaining butter. Crack an egg into each dish and season.

Cover each dish with foil and bake in the oven for 10 minutes, or until the white has set to your liking. Spoon the mushroom sauce over the egg whites and serve immediately.

SERVES 4

80G BUTTER, SOFTENED

120–150G WILD MUSHROOMS, CLEANED AND CUT INTO BITE-SIZED CHUNKS

300ML DOUBLE CREAM

SALT AND FRESHLY GROUND BLACK PEPPER

2 TBSP CHOPPED PARSLEY

4 DUCK'S EGGS

- - - - - - - - - - - - - - -

Duck's eggs are becoming more available in supermarkets these days, but if you are having problems you could always switch them for hen's eggs instead.

- - - - - - - - - - - - - - -

Baked celeriac

Preheat the oven to 200°C/gas mark 6.

If the celeriac heads still have their leafy tops attached, remove and chop finely.

Arrange the celeriac heads on an oven tray, put in the oven and cook for 1–1½ hours, turning a few times while they are cooking, until they feel tender to the point of a knife or skewer. Remove from the oven and leave for a minute or two to cool a little.

To serve, cut off the tops, roughly mash the flesh with butter, scatter over the parsley or chopped celeriac leaves and season. Alternatively, make random cuts through the flesh and just add the butter, parsley or celeriac leaves and seasoning before replacing the tops.

SERVES 4–8

2 X 600–700G CELERIAC HEADS (PREFERABLY WITH LEAFY TOPS ATTACHED)

A COUPLE OF GOOD KNOBS OF BUTTER

A FEW HANDFULS OF FLAT-LEAF PARSLEY, CHOPPED (OPTIONAL)

SALT AND FRESHLY GROUND BLACK PEPPER

- - - - - - - - - - - - - - -

This excellent sharing dish, which looks great served in the middle of the table, is one that my friend Julian Biggs created for an arty dinner last year. The original recipe called for the celeriac to be encased in salt pastry, but because of the celeriac's thick skin this works well just simply baked and turned over every so often.

- - - - - - - - - - - - - - -

Slow-baked tomatoes with Blue Monday

Preheat the oven to 120°C/gas mark 1.

Halve the tomatoes lengthways, cutting through the core, before cutting in half again. Lay the tomato quarters, cut-side up, on a baking tray lined with lightly oiled greaseproof paper. Brush over a tablespoon of the olive oil, scatter over the thyme and sea salt and season with black pepper.

Transfer to the oven and cook for about 2–3 hours, until the tomatoes have reduced in size by about half. (Some ovens – especially those that aren't fan-assisted – may take longer.) Leave to cool a little.

To serve, arrange the tomatoes on serving plates, crumble over the Blue Monday and scatter over the basil leaves. Mix the remaining oil and the vinegar together and spoon over to finish.

SERVES 4 AS A STARTER

10 MEDIUM-SIZED MIXED TOMATOES

4 TBSP EXTRA VIRGIN OLIVE OIL

2 TSP CHOPPED THYME LEAVES

1 TSP SEA SALT

FRESHLY GROUND BLACK PEPPER

150G BLUE MONDAY OR OTHER SOFT BLUE CHEESE

A SMALL HANDFUL OF GREEK BASIL LEAVES OR OTHER FRESH HERBS

½ TBSP GOOD-QUALITY RED WINE OR BALSAMIC VINEGAR

- -

Slow baking is a great way of using up a glut of tomatoes you have grown, or cheap ones bought from the market. Once they are cooked you can preserve them in sterilised Kilner-type jars with olive oil, thyme, oregano or basil, before using them chopped or blended into pasta sauces. Here I've combined a few different varieties with my favourite British blue cheese, Blue Monday – which is made in Scotland by Ruaraidh Stone – to make this great antipasti, starter, or side dish.

- -

Stuffed baked onions

Preheat the oven to 200°C/gas mark 6.

Wrap the onions in foil, stand them on a baking tray and cook for about 45–50 minutes, or until they are fairly soft. Remove from the oven, take off the foil and leave to cool a little.

Meantime, prepare the stuffing. Melt the butter in a frying pan. Season the pork with the salt, pepper and ground cumin, add to the pan and fry over a medium heat for a few minutes, stirring, until lightly coloured. Add the water and simmer gently for about 10 minutes or until the water has evaporated. Transfer to a bowl and leave to cool.

Once the onions are cool enough to handle, chop about 1cm off the tops of each, then carefully remove the skins, keeping the onions intact. Scoop out the centre of each onion with a spoon, leaving a couple of layers of flesh to hold them together. Reserve both the onion tops and scooped flesh.

Finely chop the scooped onion flesh and mix it together with the pork, breadcrumbs and parsley. Season to taste. Spoon the filling into the onions and replace the tops. Place on a baking tray, brush with oil and bake for about 15–20 minutes, until the onions are lightly coloured and the filling is hot.

SERVES 4

4 MEDIUM-SIZED RED ONIONS, PEELED

A GOOD KNOB OF BUTTER

80G FATTY MINCED PORK

SALT AND FRESHLY GROUND BLACK PEPPER

2 TSP GROUND CUMIN

120ML WATER

30G FRESH WHITE BREADCRUMBS

2 TBSP CHOPPED PARSLEY

A LITTLE VEGETABLE OR CORN OIL, FOR BRUSHING

- - - - - - - - - - - -

These stuffed onions are a good starter, though they also make a great accompaniment to roast meats, in which case you may want to stuff them with some trimmings from your joint instead. You could also try stuffing them with veal or chicken or make them vegetarian by adding some grated mature Cheddar in place of the meat.

- - - - - - - - - - - -

Root vegetable gratin

Cut the carrots, swede, parsnip and celeriac into rough 2cm chunks. Preheat the oven to 180°C/gas mark 4.

Melt the butter in a pan, add the onion and garlic and cook gently for 2–3 minutes, until soft. Add the cream, bring to the boil and season to taste. Stir in 120g of the grated cheese.

Arrange the vegetable chunks in an oven-proof serving dish and pour over the hot cream mixture.

Place the gratin dish in the centre of a deep roasting tin. Fill the tin with boiling water to halfway up the sides of the gratin dish (this will act as a bain-marie, or water bath) and transfer carefully to the oven. Bake for 45 minutes, or until the vegetables are tender to the point of a knife.

Mix the remaining cheese with the breadcrumbs, scatter over the top of the gratin and continue cooking for another 15–20 minutes, until browned.

SERVES 4–6

2 MEDIUM CARROTS, PEELED

1 SMALL SWEDE, PEELED

1 MEDIUM PARSNIP, PEELED

1 SMALL CELERIAC, PEELED

A GOOD KNOB OF BUTTER

1 LARGE ONION, PEELED, HALVED AND FINELY CHOPPED

2 GARLIC CLOVES, PEELED AND CRUSHED

1 LITRE SINGLE CREAM

SALT AND FRESHLY GROUND BLACK PEPPER

150G MATURE CHEDDAR, GRATED

60G FRESH WHITE BREADCRUMBS

- -

This dish, similar to a classic potato dish we used to make at college, is a good alternative way of serving winter roots when you've bored of boiling and roasting them. You can use any root veg you can lay your hands on here, or even try adding a few leeks, if you like.

- -

Truffled pointed cabbage

Preheat the oven to 240°C/gas mark 8. Place a pizza stone or baking tray in the oven to heat up for 20 minutes.

Halve the cabbage, season with salt and pepper and place it cut-side down on your preheated stone or tray. Bake for 10 minutes, turn over the cabbage pieces, spoon over the butter and bake for a further 15–20 minutes, or until the cabbage is tender to the point of a knife. If it looks like the cabbage might be colouring too much during cooking, cover it with foil.

To serve, place on a warmed serving plate, spoon over the truffle oil and shave over the fresh black or white truffle.

SERVES 2–4

1 POINTED CABBAGE, WASHED

SALT AND FRESHLY GROUND BLACK PEPPER

60G MELTED BUTTER

50–60ML GOOD-QUALITY TRUFFLE OIL

20–30G FRESH BLACK OR WHITE TRUFFLE

I first had this dish when Nobu opened in Mayfair. My mate Mark Edwards was experimenting with his new wood-burning oven and brought out this fantastic pointed green cabbage, also known as hispi or sweetheart cabbage. A wood-fired oven is the key to getting this dish perfect, but you'll get a pretty good result if you cook it on a pizza stone in a red-hot oven. You can use black or white truffles for this depending on your budget, and be aware that some of those truffle oils you see on sale are chemically flavoured and not the real thing. Use a mandolin or specialised truffle slicer for shaving the truffles - even the sharpest of knives doesn't really do the job.

SAVOURY PIES, TARTS ETC.

Asparagus tart

Roll out the puff pastry on a lightly floured surface to a 3mm thickness. Cut the pastry into 4 rectangles about 11 x 7cm and prick them all over with a fork, then lay them on a baking tray. With the point of a knife, mark a line all the way round the rectangles about 3mm from the edge. Brush the edges with beaten egg, and leave to rest in the fridge for 1 hour.

Cut the top 10cm of the asparagus spears from the tip, reserving the stalks. Bring two pans of salted water to the boil. Cook the spears for 3–4 minutes until tender, then drain and refresh in cold water to stop them discolouring.

Cook the trimmings in the other pan for about 7–8 minutes until soft, then drain and whiz in a blender or food processor with the grated cheese and half of the butter to a coarse purée. Season with salt and pepper to taste.

Preheat the oven to 200°C/gas mark 6.

Cut 4 rectangles out of cardboard just large enough to cover the centre of the tarts but not the marked edges. Wrap each in tin foil and place in the centre of the tarts. Bake the pastry cases for about 8–10 minutes, or until the edges are golden.

Remove the foil rectangles and spread a tablespoon or so of the asparagus purée in the middle of each tart. Don't put in too much (save what you have left to use as a dip). Lay the asparagus spears as close together as possible on top of the purée. Season the asparagus with salt and pepper and bake for a further 5–6 minutes. Melt the remaining butter, brush over the asparagus and serve immediately.

SERVES 4

200G READY-MADE ALL-BUTTER PUFF PASTRY

PLAIN FLOUR, FOR DUSTING

1 EGG, BEATEN

500G MEDIUM ASPARAGUS, WOODY ENDS REMOVED

30G MATURE CHEDDAR, GRATED

60G BUTTER

SALT AND FRESHLY GROUND BLACK PEPPER

- - - - - - - - - - - - - - - - - - - -
This makes a delicious snack or starter for a lunch or dinner party. It's also good with a little extra hard cheese like Parmesan shaved over the top or with hollandaise (see page 56) — that perfect partner for asparagus — spooned over it.
- - - - - - - - - - - - - - - - - - - -

Celeriac and Lancashire cheese pithivier

Melt the butter in a pan, add the onion and gently cook for 2–3 minutes without colouring. Remove from the heat and leave to cool.

Cut the celeriac in half and slice it as thinly as possible with a very sharp knife or mandolin. Blanch the slices in boiling salted water for 2–3 minutes.

Roll out the pastry on a lightly floured surface to a 1cm thickness and cut it out into two discs, one about 25cm across and the other about 30cm. Lay the smaller one on a tray and prick holes in it with a fork. Arrange a layer of the celeriac slices over the pastry, leaving a 2cm margin around the edge. Scatter over some onion, a little cheese and season, then add another layer of celeriac slices. Continue layering up the ingredients in this fashion until you have used them all up.

Brush the edges of the pastry with egg and lay the larger pastry disc on top, pressing the edges together with your fingers. You can decorate the pithivier by making lines with the back of a small knife from the centre of the pastry if you wish. Brush with egg and leave to rest in the fridge for 30 minutes. Preheat the oven to 180°C/gas mark 4.

Bake the pithivier for about 30–40 minutes until golden. Serve.

SERVES 6–8

A COUPLE OF GOOD KNOBS OF BUTTER

1 MEDIUM ONION, PEELED, HALVED AND FINELY CHOPPED

1 X 400–500G CELERIAC, PEELED

SALT AND FRESHLY GROUND BLACK PEPPER

250–300G READY-MADE ALL-BUTTER PUFF PASTRY

PLAIN FLOUR, FOR DUSTING

200G LANCASHIRE CHEESE, GRATED

1 EGG, BEATEN

If this sounds like some kind of vegetarian main course at a dinner party, well, it pretty much is, and I'm sure most vegetarians would be really happy to be served a slice of this. You could even get away with serving it to non-vegetarians – it would sit nicely at the table for a buffet, while a slice would be great with a piece of roast lamb.

Cold veal and ham pie

To make the pastry, mix the flour and salt in a bowl and make a well in the centre. Bring the water and lard to the boil in a saucepan then stir it into the flour with a wooden spoon to form a smooth dough. Cover and leave for 15 minutes or so until the dough is cooler, less sticky and easier to handle.

Preheat the oven to 200°C/gas mark 6.

For the filling, heat the butter in a pan, add the onion and gently cook, covered, for 3–4 minutes until soft. Finely chop or mince a fifth of the veal and ham (you could do this in a food processor), mix with the softened onion and parsley, and season. Slice the remaining ham into rough 5–8mm slices and season lightly. Put the rest of the veal between 2 sheets of cling film and bat them out with a rolling pin or meat bat to roughly the same thickness as the ham. Season lightly.

Lightly grease a raised pie mould, 20 x 5cm deep flan ring or loose-bottomed cake tin and line the bottom with a disc of lightly greased silicone or greaseproof paper. Place it on a lined baking tray.

Transfer two-thirds of the dough to a lightly floured table and roll it into a circle to a 5mm thickness and 26cm diameter. Making sure there are no holes in the pastry, place the dough into your ring or mould and carefully press

SERVES 4

A GOOD KNOB OF BUTTER

1 ONION, PEELED AND FINELY CHOPPED

450G BONED WEIGHT OF VEAL, CUT INTO SLICES

450G HAM HOCK, COOKED (SEE PAGE 114), RESERVING 300ML OF THE HAM STOCK

4 TBSP CHOPPED PARSLEY

SALT AND FRESHLY GROUND BLACK PEPPER

3 GELATINE LEAVES

FOR THE HOT-WATER PASTRY

375G PLAIN FLOUR

½ TSP SALT

150ML WATER

130G LARD

1 EGG, BEATEN

Traditional pies make the perfect picnic food, and if you make your own large pie everyone gets a slice with lots of filling and less pastry than with individual pies. If you're not a confident cook, pies like this can seem tricky to make, but believe me, they're no harder than most desserts. Once you've made one a couple of times you can adapt the filling according to your preference and what you have to hand, using ingredients such as chicken, mushrooms or at Christmas time turkey, ham and cranberry.

into the corners, allowing the excess to just hang over the edge. Roll out the rest of the pastry to the diameter of your ring, tin or pie mould to make the pie lid. Cut a 2cm hole in the centre of the pastry.

Cover the bottom of your dish first with a layer of ham then a layer of veal, breaking or cutting the meat to fill the gaps as necessary. Follow this with all the chopped veal and ham mixture, pressing it down firmly. Top with a final layer of ham then veal and finish by carefully laying the pastry lid on top. Trim the edges of the pastry with a knife and pinch the base and top pastry edges together with your forefinger and thumb to make a good join.

Brush the top of the pie all over with the beaten egg, transfer to the oven and cook for 45 minutes. If it is colouring too much, cover with foil and turn the oven down slightly.

Remove the pastry from its ring or tin and brush the sides and top again with egg before baking for a further 15 minutes until nicely coloured. Remove from the oven and leave to cool, then chill for a couple of hours. Check around the pastry for any holes, filling them with a little softened butter.

Meanwhile, soak the gelatine leaves in cold water to cover for a few minutes until they soften. Bring 60ml of the reserved ham stock to a simmer. Remove the stock from the heat, squeeze the gelatine leaves to remove excess water, then add to the hot stock and stir until fully dissolved. Stir this into a further 240ml of ham stock and leave to cool, but do not let it set.

Pour about a third of the stock into the round hole in the top of the pastry a little at a time until it's all used up. The pie will keep for about a week in the fridge. Serve cold with Cumberland sauce, piccalilli or your favourite chutney or relish.

Crab and seashore vegetable tart

Roll out the pastry on a floured table to about 2mm thick. Use to line four individual tart tins 10cm in diameter and 2–3cm deep. Using your thumb and forefinger, firm the pastry up to – and a little over – the top of the tins. Prick the pastry all over with a fork, then line the tarts with greaseproof paper or foil and fill with baking beans. Refrigerate for 1 hour.

Preheat the oven to 180°C/gas mark 4.

Bake the cases for 20 minutes, then remove the baking beans and paper and return to the oven for 5 minutes until lightly golden. Remove from the tins and leave on a wire rack to cool.

Meantime, simmer the fish stock and vermouth in a pan until reduced to about a tablespoon in volume. Add the double cream and continue simmering until it has thickened and reduced by half. Add the brown crab meat, if using, and blend with a hand blender or in a liquidiser until smooth.

Add the seashore vegetables to a pan of boiling water and cook for a minute, so they are still a little firm to the bite. Drain. Add to the sauce with the white crab meat, season to taste and heat gently to warm through. Return the tart cases to the oven for a minute or two to warm. Remove from the oven and spoon the crab mixture into the cases. Flash under a hot grill until lightly coloured to finish, or serve as they are.

SERVES 4

250–300G READY-MADE ALL-BUTTER PUFF PASTRY

PLAIN FLOUR, FOR DUSTING

200ML FISH STOCK

60ML WHITE VERMOUTH

250ML DOUBLE CREAM

1 TBSP BROWN CRAB MEAT (OPTIONAL)

A HANDFUL OF SEASHORE VEGETABLES (SEA BEET, SEA PURSLANE, SEA ASTER, SAMPHIRE ETC.), WASHED, TRIMMED AND ROUGHLY CHOPPED

150G FRESHLY PICKED WHITE CRAB MEAT

SALT AND FRESHLY GROUND BLACK PEPPER

- -

A deliciously rich savoury starter, lunch or tea-time snack. Because you bake these tarts blind they shouldn't rise, leaving you with a light, crisp case that can be used for sweet or savoury dishes. Ideally the meat from a freshly cooked crab is best for this, with a little of the brown meat blended into the sauce to enrich it. If you don't have a fresh crab handy, just buy the best quality fresh white crab meat you can find.

- -

Oyster and chorizo pies

Prise open the oysters. Lay an oyster in a folded tea towel on a surface with the flat shell uppermost and the pointed hinge facing towards you. Holding the oyster down with the cloth, force the tip of an oyster knife into the hinge of the shell, carefully moving it from side to side until you can feel the shell loosening – it will take some force.

Keeping the knife in the shell, twist it a little and run it along the top of the shell until you feel the muscle, which attaches the oyster to the shell. Cut through this to detach the top shell. Remove any bits of shell that may be on the oyster flesh, but don't pour away the natural juices. Set aside.

Heat a frying pan and gently cook the chorizo and shallots for 3–4 minutes over a low heat. Add the water and the oyster juices and simmer for a further minute before removing from the heat. Leave to cool. Once cool, spoon the chorizo mixture over the oysters.

Roll out the pastry on a floured table to about 2mm thick. Cut the pastry just slightly larger than the shells and brush the edges with the beaten egg. Cover the oysters with the pastry, egg washed side down, pressing the edges to the shell to fix them in place. Brush the top and sides of the pastry with more beaten egg, place them on a tray and leave to rest in the fridge until required. Preheat the oven to 220°C/gas mark 7.

Bake for about 12–15 minutes until golden. Make little piles of rock salt on the centre of each serving plate and lightly press an oyster pie into each to stop them from wobbling around. Serve immediately.

SERVES 4

4 VERY LARGE OYSTERS

70–80G COOKING CHORIZO, FINELY CHOPPED

2 MEDIUM SHALLOTS, PEELED, HALVED AND FINELY CHOPPED

2–3 TBSP WATER

100G READY-MADE ALL-BUTTER PUFF PASTRY

1 EGG, BEATEN

ROCK SALT, TO SERVE

- -

Occasionally we get a few enormous oysters in the restaurant that are way too big to swallow raw and are only good for cooking. They make perfect, natural little pies. At home, you'll probably need to order in these large oysters in advance from your fishmonger. There are several other flavourings you could slip under their pastry lids – bacon, shallots and a little cream would work equally well, for example.

- -

Ham hock, snail and wild garlic pie

Place the ham hock in a large pan with half the onions, the peppercorns and bay leaf. Cover with cold water and bring to the boil, then lower the heat and simmer for 1½ –2 hours, or until tender. Remove the hock from the pan, reserving the liquid, and leave to cool. Once cool, remove and discard any skin and remove the meat from the bone. Reserve the bone, cut the meat into rough 3cm chunks and put to one side. Strain the liquid through a fine strainer, measure out a litre and add to a pan over a low heat to keep hot.

Finely chop the remaining onion halves, add to a heavy-based saucepan with the butter and cook for 2–3 minutes until soft. Add the flour and stir well. Gradually add the white wine, stirring to avoid any lumps. Then add the reserved ham stock, stirring, bit by bit. Bring to the boil and simmer gently for 30 minutes. The sauce should be quite thick by now – if not, continue simmering for a little longer. Remove from the heat and leave to cool a little. Add the ham hock meat, snails and garlic and season to taste. Fill a large pie dish with the mixture.

For the pastry, mix the flour, salt and suet together in a bowl. Add the butter and rub with your fingertips until you have a fine breadcrumb-like consistency. Mix in the water to form a smooth dough, then knead for a minute.

Roll the pastry out on a lightly floured surface to about a 7mm thickness. Trim until about 2cm larger all the way round than the rim of your pie dish. Place the ham bone in the centre of the pie. Brush the edges of the pastry with a little of the beaten egg, make a slit in the centre for the bone and lay the pastry on top of your pie, pressing the egg-washed edges onto the rim of the dish. Brush the top of the pastry with beaten egg and leave to rest in a cool place for about 30 minutes.

Preheat the oven to 180°C/gas mark 4. Bake for about 45 minutes, or until the pastry is golden brown. Serve at once.

SERVES 4

1 X 700G–1KG HAM HOCK

4 MEDIUM ONIONS, PEELED AND HALVED

1 TSP BLACK PEPPERCORNS

1 BAY LEAF

70G BUTTER

60G FLOUR

100ML WHITE WINE

16–20 PLUMP COOKED SNAILS, SHELLS REMOVED

A HANDFUL OF WILD GARLIC, CHOPPED (OR GARLIC CHIVES)

SALT AND FRESHLY GROUND BLACK PEPPER

1 EGG, BEATEN

FOR THE PASTRY

225G SELF-RAISING FLOUR

1 TSP SALT

85G SHREDDED BEEF SUET

60G BUTTER, CHILLED AND COARSELY GRATED

150–175ML WATER

PLAIN FLOUR, FOR DUSTING

- -

We tend to associate cooking snails with France and Spain but there is a snail eating culture in Britain which dates back about 2000 years, although there are no specific British recipes for snails like in France. I've used them in various ways with, say, wild rabbit cooked in cider, as a soup garnish and in pies like this. Though you can purify your own garden snails, it's a bit fiddly, so I suggest you use bought cooked ones here.

- -

Macaroni pie

Preheat the oven to 180°C/gas mark 4.

Roll out the pastry on a floured table to about 2mm thick. Lightly grease a 25 x 3cm deep loose-bottomed flan tin, line it with the pastry and trim the edges. Line with foil or greaseproof paper, fill with a layer of baking beans and bake blind for 15 minutes. Remove the greaseproof paper and beans and bake for a further 6–7 minutes, until the pastry is lightly golden. Remove from the oven. Turn the oven up to 220°C/gas mark 7.

Meantime, melt the mascarpone in a thick-bottomed pan with 150g of the Cheddar and bring it to the boil. Add the double cream, season with salt and pepper and simmer for a couple of minutes until it thickens. Whisk the sauce well and mix with the cooked pasta.

Put the macaroni mixture into the flan case and scatter over the remaining Cheddar. Bake for 20–25 minutes, until nicely browned. Serve immediately.

SERVES 4

200–250G READY-MADE SHORT-CRUST PASTRY

PLAIN FLOUR, FOR DUSTING

BUTTER, FOR GREASING

300G MASCARPONE CHEESE

170G MATURE CHEDDAR, FINELY GRATED

150ML DOUBLE CREAM

SALT AND FRESHLY GROUND BLACK PEPPER

150G MACARONI, COOKED ACCORDING TO PACKET INSTRUCTIONS

I had something like this in Barbados some years ago which was delicious. I don't think it's a native Bajan recipe, but is more likely something that has made its way over from the States. Serve this extremely rich pie with a few dressed green salad leaves. It really doesn't need anything else.

Pheasant b'stilla

Cut the legs from the pheasant, then cut through the leg joint to separate the thigh from the drumstick. Remove the skin from the thighs and cut out the bone with the point of a sharp knife. Cut the breasts away from the carcass and remove the skin. Cut the thigh and breast meat into rough 2cm chunks and place in a bowl.

Chop the drumsticks and carcass into small pieces using a heavy chopping knife or cleaver. Bring the chicken stock to a simmer in a large pan, add the chopped bones and gently simmer for 45 minutes. Skim any froth from the surface, strain through a fine-meshed sieve and discard the bones. Preheat the oven to 200°C/gas mark 6.

Heat the oil in a heavy-bottomed pan, add the pheasant meat and fry until nicely coloured, stirring occasionally. Add the onion, garlic, saffron, ginger, pepper and salt and stir well. Pour in the stock, bring to the boil and simmer very gently for 30 minutes. Add the icing sugar and 100g butter and simmer for another 20 minutes. The meat should be tender and the cooking liquid reduced to a few tablespoons. If not, simmer a little longer. Break the meat up a little into the sauce with a spoon, add the coriander and leave to cool.

To assemble the b'stilla, take a straight-sided tart or cake tin with a removable bottom (or a bottomless flan ring on a baking tray) measuring 18–20cm across by 5– 6cm deep. Melt the remaining butter and use to brush the bottom and sides. Lay a sheet of filo on the base. Then lay another 10 sheets all round the tin, overlapping the central sheet on the base and going up the sides of the tin so that half of each sheet overhangs the tin's edge.

Mix the sugared-almond mixture ingredients together in a bowl. Spread half the mix on the base of the pastry, leaving about 1cm around the edges. Place 2 more sheets of pastry over the almond mixture. Add the chopped eggs with

SERVES 4

1 PHEASANT

1 LITRE CHICKEN STOCK

6 TBSP OLIVE OIL

1 MEDIUM ONION, PEELED, HALVED AND FINELY CHOPPED

4 GARLIC CLOVES, PEELED AND CRUSHED

A GOOD PINCH OF SAFFRON

1 TSP POWDERED GINGER

1 TSP FRESHLY GROUND BLACK PEPPER

1 TSP SALT

1 TBSP ICING SUGAR, PLUS EXTRA FOR DUSTING

160G BUTTER

1 TBSP CHOPPED CORIANDER

ABOUT 20–24 WARKA OR FILO PASTRY SHEETS MEASURING ABOUT 18CM SQUARE

5 HARD-BOILED EGGS, CHOPPED

GROUND CINNAMON, FOR DUSTING

FOR THE SUGARED-ALMOND MIXTURE

350G GROUND ALMONDS

5 TBSP ICING SUGAR

3 TBSP ORANGE BLOSSOM WATER OR 4 TBSP WATER

½ TSP GROUND CINNAMON

If you've been to Morocco you may have come across b'stilla, pronounced and sometimes spelt pastilla. It's traditionally made with pigeon and is a sort of sweet and savoury pie using sugar and almonds which were probably originally used to disguise the birds' gaminess. I normally make it with pheasants as they are plentiful in game season and less fiddly to prepare, though chicken works well too.

the pheasant mixture and spoon over the pastry. Cover with an additional 2 pastry sheets. Spoon the remaining almond mixture over the pastry then cover with another 3 or 4 pastry sheets. Brush with more butter and fold the overhanging sides up and towards the middle before covering with a final pastry sheet. Using your hands, gently press down upon the top to finish.

Bake the b'stilla in the preheated oven for about 20 minutes, until golden brown. Remove from the oven and carefully run a knife around the edge to loosen the sides. Place a serving dish or flat plate upside down over the tin, carefully invert the b'stilla onto the plate and slide it onto a baking tray. Brush all over with melted butter, return to the oven and cook for a further 15 minutes until golden, turning the oven down or covering with foil if it looks as though it is colouring too rapidly.

Remove the b'stilla from the oven and leave to cool a little. Using a fish slice, carefully transfer to a serving dish. Cut some long strips of paper about 1cm wide. Dust the top with icing sugar before laying over the paper strips a couple of centimetres apart. Dredge with the cinnamon before removing the strips to create a lattice pattern. Serve.

My hangover tarte Dijonnaise

Preheat the oven to 200°C/gas mark 6. Roll out the pastry on a floured table to about 3mm thick. Lay the puff pastry on a deep baking tray and prick it all over with a fork. Bake for 8–10 minutes, or until lightly coloured.

Meanwhile gently cook the onion and peppers in the olive oil for 4–5 minutes, covered and stirring occasionally, until soft. Remove from the heat and leave to cool. Add the pepper mixture to a bowl with the cheese, eggs, cream and mustard, stir to combine and season to taste. Carefully turn the pastry over in the tray and spread the mixture over. Bake for 15 minutes until lightly coloured and serve warm on its own or with a salad.

SERVES 4–6 AS A SNACK

250G READY-MADE ALL-BUTTER PUFF PASTRY

1 ONION, PEELED AND FINELY CHOPPED

2 RED OR GREEN PEPPERS, SEEDED AND CUT INTO ROUGH 1CM STRIPS

2 TBSP OLIVE OIL

80G GRATED MEDIUM CHEDDAR

2 EGGS, BEATEN

2 TBSP DOUBLE CREAM

2 TSP DIJON MUSTARD

SALT AND FRESHLY GROUND BLACK PEPPER

- -

I sometimes get a craving for this tangy mustardy tart, especially if I've had a late night. Another version can be made with red peppers and fresh thyme or oregano leaves. Spread the pepper and onion mixture onto the pastry as above, dot some pieces of goat's cheese around the pastry and bake as before until golden brown.

- -

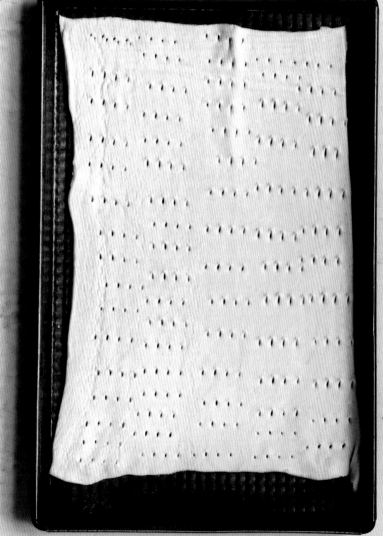

Spanakopita

Heat the olive oil in a large saucepan, add the onions and cinnamon and cook gently for 2–3 minutes, until the onions are soft. Add the spinach, cover with a lid and cook for a few minutes, stirring occasionally, until wilted (you may need to add the spinach in batches). Transfer to a colander, drain and leave to cool. Mix the cooled spinach with the tomatoes and rice in a bowl and season to taste. Preheat the oven to 200°C/gas mark 6.

Lay a sheet of filo on a floured work surface and brush with a little melted butter. Lay another filo sheet on top and brush with more butter before repeat with the remaining sheets. Spoon the spinach mixture along the long edge of the filo and roll up into a sausage shape. Butter a large round cake tin or a large oven-proof frying pan. Carefully roll the pastry into a coil and place on the tin or in the pan. Brush with butter all over, transfer to the oven and bake for 25–30 minutes until the pastry is crisp. Serve hot or warm.

SERVES 4–6

2 TBSP OLIVE OIL

2 ONIONS, PEELED, HALVED AND FINELY CHOPPED

½ TSP GROUND CINNAMON

500G SPINACH, TRIMMED AND WASHED

2 LARGE TOMATOES, FINELY CHOPPED

40G SHORT-GRAIN RICE, COOKED ACCORDING TO PACKET INSTRUCTIONS

SALT AND FRESHLY GROUND BLACK PEPPER

4 SHEETS OF FILO PASTRY

PLAIN FLOUR, FOR DUSTING

30G BUTTER, MELTED

- -

There are many variations of this classic Greek spinach-filled pie, with the casing varying from filo pastry to yeast-based crusts and the shape from the traditional square or rectangular pie to a snake-like shape like this.

- -

Timpano with spring leeks and wild mushrooms

Heat the butter in a large pan, add the pancetta and gently cook for 3–4 minutes without colouring. Add the flour and cook, stirring, for a minute or so, before gradually stirring in the milk and chicken stock. Bring to the boil, season and simmer gently for about 30 minutes, giving the mixture an occasional whisk to prevent lumps forming, until it's thick.

Meanwhile, heat the oil in a pan, add the leeks and gently cook for 3–4 minutes, covered, until soft. Add the mushrooms, cover again and continue cooking for a further 3–4 minutes, until the mushrooms have softened. Add the wild garlic leaves and continue to cook for a minute, stirring, before adding to the pancetta mixture along with the macaroni, cream and Parmesan. Mix well and season to taste if necessary. Preheat the oven to 180°C/gas mark 4.

Brush an oven-proof pudding basin or large dish with olive oil. Scatter it with the breadcrumbs then line it with the lasagne sheets, leaving some overlapping the bowl to fold over the top.

Pour the macaroni mixture into the lined dish and fold over the lasagne sheets. Cover with foil and bake for 45 minutes.

To serve, turn out carefully onto a warmed plate and cut into wedges.

SERVES 4–6

40G BUTTER

80G PANCETTA, OR STREAKY BACON CUT INTO ½ CM DICE

30G FLOUR

300ML HOT MILK

300ML HOT CHICKEN STOCK

SALT AND FRESHLY GROUND BLACK PEPPER

2 TBSP OLIVE OIL, PLUS EXTRA FOR OILING

2–3 YOUNG LEEKS, OR 4–5 BABY LEEKS, SHREDDED

200G WILD MUSHROOMS, CLEANED, WASHED IF NECESSARY AND DRIED

A HANDFUL OF WILD GARLIC LEAVES, TORN

120G MACARONI, COOKED ACCORDING TO PACKET INSTRUCTIONS

2–3 TBSP DOUBLE CREAM

40G FRESHLY GRATED PARMESAN

3–4 TBSP FRESH WHITE BREADCRUMBS, LIGHTLY TOASTED

7 LASAGNE SHEETS, COOKED ACCORDING TO PACKET INSTRUCTIONS

- -
A bit like a savoury cake, this is a great dish to serve for a festive occasion. I first made this with Giorgio Locatelli when we did the Berkeley Square Ball charity dinner together. It was a big affair and we did an unheard of family-style dinner where the 700 or so guests helped themselves from the centre of the table.
- -

SWEET PIES,
TARTS ETC.

Pumpkin pie

First make the pastry. In a food processor, electric mixer or by hand, beat the butter and sugar together until smooth and creamy. Slowly mix in the beaten egg (scraping the sides of the bowl every so often if you are using a mixer), then gradually fold in the flour to form a smooth dough. Shape into a ball, wrap in cling film and refrigerate for 30 minutes.

Lightly grease a 25 x 4cm deep tart tin. Roll out the pastry on a floured table to about 3mm thick and cut out a disc just large enough to line the tin. This pastry is quite delicate, but forgiving – if it starts breaking up on you, just patch it up when lining the tin and mould it back together with your fingers. Neaten up the edges of the pastry by pinching with your thumb and forefinger all the way around, then leave to rest for 1 hour in the fridge.

Meanwhile, make the filling. Preheat the oven to 190°C/gas mark 5. Put the pumpkin pieces on a roasting tray with the mixed spice and butter. Cover with foil and bake for 45 minutes until soft, stirring occasionally. Drain and cool in a colander, then blend in a liquidiser until smooth. Push the mix through a conical strainer, colander or sieve to remove any fibrous strands.

Bring the cream to the boil, mix with the sugar and stir until dissolved. Add to the blender with the egg and puréed pumpkin and blend until smooth.

Turn the oven down to 150°C/gas mark 2. Remove the pastry from the fridge, line with greaseproof paper and fill with baking beans. Bake blind for 10–15 minutes, until the pastry is lightly golden. Remove the beans and paper and leave to rest for 5 minutes. Pour the pumpkin mix up to the top of the tart case and bake for a further 30 minutes, or until the filling has set.

To serve, put the pumpkin seeds on some foil on a baking tray, dust with icing sugar and bake in the oven for 10 minutes or so until golden. Carefully cut the pie into slices and scatter the seeds over the top. Serve as it is or with crème fraîche or mascarpone.

SERVES 6–8

125G UNSALTED BUTTER, PLUS EXTRA FOR GREASING

180G CASTER SUGAR

1 LARGE EGG, BEATEN

250G PLAIN FLOUR, PLUS EXTRA FOR DUSTING

A FEW HANDFULS OF PUMPKIN SEEDS

ICING SUGAR, FOR DUSTING

FOR THE FILLING

700G ORANGE-FLESHED, RIPE PUMPKIN OR BUTTERNUT SQUASH, PEELED, SEEDED AND CUT INTO ROUGH CHUNKS

½ TSP MIXED SPICE

60G BUTTER

200ML DOUBLE CREAM

150G CASTER SUGAR

1 SMALL EGG, BEATEN

- -

This is a more accessible version of the American classic. Try to find a ripe orange-fleshed pumpkin if you can, though you can always use a butternut squash instead - they tend to be pretty consistent in terms of their flavour and ripeness.

- -

Tarte à la crème

Roll out the pastry on a floured table to about 4mm thick. Use to line four individual 10 x 2cm deep tart cases. Prick all over with a fork and cover with greaseproof paper or foil, then line with baking beans. Leave to rest in the fridge for 1 hour.

Preheat the oven to 180°C/gas mark 4.

Bake the tart cases for 15 minutes, then remove the baking beans and paper and cook for a further 5 minutes. Remove from the oven and leave to rest for 5 minutes before removing the pastry cases from the tins.

Meanwhile, put the cream in a saucepan with the sugar, vanilla pod and seeds. Bring to the boil and simmer gently, stirring with a whisk every so often, for about 5 minutes, or until the mixture has reduced by half. Discard the vanilla pods, fill the tarts with the mixture and leave to set in the fridge. Serve with berries.

SERVES 4

200G READY-MADE ALL-BUTTER PUFF PASTRY

700ML UHT DOUBLE CREAM

70G CASTER SUGAR

1 VANILLA POD, SPLIT AND SEEDS SCRAPED OUT

- - - - - - - - - - -

The French equivalent of a custard tart, this hits the spot as either a simple but indulgent dessert or afternoon tea pastry. The French don't have the type of fresh double cream we have, with much of theirs being long-life instead. To get the flavour of the tart to match those found in France you need to use the same.

- - - - - - - - - - -

Saffron custard tarts

Roll out the pastry on a lightly floured work surface to a 3mm thickness and prick it thoroughly all over with a fork. Fold loosely in half and leave to rest in the fridge for 30–40 minutes.

Have ready a 12-hole muffin tray. Unfold the pastry and cut out circles, using a 9–10cm cutter. Use these to line the muffin tins, pushing the pastry into the corners before trimming the tops neatly with a sharp knife. Line each with a disc of greaseproof paper or foil, add baking beans and leave to rest in the fridge for 15 minutes. Preheat the oven to 180°C/gas mark 4.

Bake the tart cases for 10–15 minutes until they begin to colour, then remove from the oven, take out the paper and baking beans and leave to cool for a few minutes.

Meanwhile, put the cream and saffron into a small saucepan and bring to the boil. Remove from the heat and leave to infuse for 10 minutes.

In a bowl, mix together the egg yolks, sugar and cornflour. Pour the infused cream over the egg mixture, stirring well with a whisk. Return to the pan and cook gently over a low heat for a few minutes, stirring constantly with a wooden spoon, until the custard thickens. Don't let it boil. Remove from the heat and transfer to a jug.

Pour the saffron custard into the tart cases and bake for 10–12 minutes, until set. Leave to cool a little, then loosen the tarts with a small knife and carefully remove from the tin. Serve warm or cold.

MAKES 10–12

250–300G READY-MADE ALL-BUTTER PUFF PASTRY

PLAIN FLOUR, FOR DUSTING

250ML SINGLE CREAM

A GOOD PINCH OF SAFFRON STRANDS

4 EGG YOLKS

50G CASTER SUGAR

1½ TSP CORNFLOUR

- -

Similar to those Portuguese custards tarts, but with added saffron, these are great little tea-time snacks. Although saffron might not seem an obvious spice for a dessert, its delicate taste lends itself to cakes and creamy fillings like this.

- -

Galette au fenouil

Roll out the pastry on a floured table to about 3mm thick. Cut the pastry into four 13cm discs and prick them all over with a fork. Leave to rest in the fridge for 1 hour.

Meantime, prepare the topping. Trim the fennel bulbs if necessary. If there is any fern on the fennel, chop it finely and put it to one side. Put the bulbs whole into a saucepan with the sugar and fennel seeds. Cover with water, bring to the boil and simmer gently for about 1 hour, until the fennel is soft to the point of a knife. Remove the bulbs from the cooking syrup, setting both aside. Preheat the oven to 200°C/gas mark 6.

Place the pastry discs on a baking tray and cover with a wire cooling rack to stop them rising while cooking. Bake for 7 minutes, then turn the discs over and cook for a further 4 minutes with the rack in place. Remove from the oven and set aside.

Strain 500ml of the cooking syrup through a fine-meshed sieve into a clean pan. Bring to the boil, lower to a simmer and cook until it has reduced to around 4 or 5 tablespoonfuls in volume. Remove from the heat and leave to cool a little before adding the chopped fennel fern or dill.

Cut the fennel bulbs lengthways into 5mm slices. To assemble the tarts, arrange the fennel slices on the puff pastry discs in a circular pattern, ensuring the fennel goes to the edges of the pastry. Dust with icing sugar and bake for 7–8 minutes until golden (cover the tarts with foil if they begin to cover too rapidly). To serve, spoon the syrup around the tarts and top with a dollop of crème fraîche.

SERVES 4

200G READY-MADE ALL-BUTTER PUFF PASTRY

PLAIN FLOUR, FOR DUSTING

1KG FENNEL

300G CASTER SUGAR

2 TSP FENNEL SEEDS

2 TSP FINELY CHOPPED DILL (IF THERE IS NO FERN ON THE FENNEL)

ICING SUGAR, FOR DUSTING

200G CRÈME FRAÎCHE

- -

This may sound like a bit of a wacky dessert, but it really is quite delicious. A pastry chef at The Ivy introduced me to it years ago and it stayed on the menu for ages. If you want to get ahead, you can cook the fennel a day or so in advance - if doing so, leave it in the syrup until needed.

- -

Torta di ricotta

Preheat the oven to 180°C/gas mark 5. Butter a 22 x 6cm deep loose-bottomed cake tin.

Mix the almonds with the chocolate in a bowl and add the eggs and sugar. Beat well, then stir in the ricotta, orange zest, cinnamon, Cointreau and baking powder until well mixed. Put to one side.

To make the base, beat the eggs with the caster sugar and olive oil in a bowl. Stir in the flour and baking powder. Spoon the base mix into the buttered cake tin, spreading it over evenly.

Pour the chocolate mixture over the base, transfer to the oven and bake for 1 hour, until the centre is just firm. Leave to cool in the tin for 10 minutes before turning out onto a cake rack. Dust with cocoa powder and serve warm or cold.

- - - - - - - - - - - - - - -

This is a nice, simple
dessert - delicious served
warm or cold and accompanied
with a few seasonal fruits
or chocolate sauce for that
bit of extra indulgence.

- - - - - - - - - - - - - - -

SERVES 8–10

BUTTER, FOR GREASING

150G GROUND ALMONDS

150G GOOD-QUALITY DARK CHOCOLATE, FINELY GRATED

4 MEDIUM EGGS, BEATEN

250G CASTER SUGAR

500G RICOTTA

FINELY GRATED ZEST OF 1 ORANGE

½ TSP GROUND CINNAMON

1 TBSP COINTREAU

2 TSP BAKING POWDER

GOOD-QUALITY COCOA POWDER, FOR DUSTING

FOR THE BASE

2 MEDIUM EGGS

50G CASTER SUGAR

4 TBSP OLIVE OIL

100G PLAIN FLOUR

1½ TSP BAKING POWDER

Damson tart with plum zabaglione

Preheat the oven to 220°C/gas mark 7.

Roll out the pastry on a floured table to about 3mm thick. Cut the pastry into four rectangles about 6 x 12cm and prick all over with a fork. Leave to rest in the fridge for 1 hour.

Arrange the damsons on the pastry cut-side down, leaving a 5mm margin around the edges. Brush them with the butter and sieve over half the sugar. Bake for 10 minutes, then sieve over the rest of the sugar and continue cooking for another 5–10 minutes, until the damsons are golden brown and caramelised.

Meantime, make the zabaglione. Put the plum spirit, egg yolks and sugar in a mixing bowl over a pan of simmering water. Whisk continuously for a few minutes until the mixture is light, fluffy and doubled in volume.

To serve, transfer the tarts to a warm plate and spoon over the zabaglione.

SERVES 4

200G READY-MADE ALL-BUTTER PUFF PASTRY

PLAIN FLOUR, FOR DUSTING

300–400G DAMSONS, GREENGAGES OR VICTORIA PLUMS, HALVED AND STONED

A COUPLE OF GOOD KNOBS OF BUTTER, MELTED

2 TBSP ICING SUGAR

FOR THE ZABAGLIONE

40ML PLUM SPIRIT OR EAU-DE-VIE

2 EGG YOLKS

1 TBSP CASTER SUGAR

- -
When plums are in season this simple, no frills tart makes for an easy dessert. You could make it with a mixture of damsons, greengages or even normal-sized plums like Victoria. When making this I had a bottle of plum spirit – a sort of local grappa – knocking around in my cupboard from a trip to Transylvania, which I used to whip up a zabaglione in keeping with the plum theme.
- -

Sweet beetroot tart

Roll out the pastry on a lightly floured surface to about 2mm thick, then cut it into four 13cm discs. Prick the discs all over with a fork and leave to rest in the fridge for 1 hour. Fold the trimmings over, wrap in cling film and keep for another recipe (the arlette biscuits on page 148, for example). Preheat the oven to 200°C/gas mark 6.

Put the discs onto a baking tray lined with silicone or greaseproof paper. Lay the beetroot slices on the pastry discs, overlapping them and tucking the last slice under the first to form an even pattern.

Brush the beetroot with a little of the melted butter and dust generously with icing sugar. Bake for about 30 minutes, or until the beetroot begins to caramelise, scattering more icing sugar and brushing over the remaining butter halfway through cooking.

Spoon a dollop of crème fraîche into the centre of each tart and serve.

SERVES 4

250–300G READY-MADE ALL-BUTTER PUFF PASTRY

6 OR SO MEDIUM-SIZED RED BEETROOT, COOKED, PEELED AND THINLY SLICED

30G BUTTER, MELTED

ICING SUGAR, FOR DUSTING

CRÈME FRAÎCHE, TO SERVE

- - - - - - - - - - - - - - -

Like the gallete au fenouil on page 132 this may seem a little bit strange, but trust me — it is not only delicious, but gloriously pretty as well. We tend to ignore using common savoury ingredients when it comes to dessert, but it's amazing how a bit of sugar can transform them.

- - - - - - - - - - - - - - -

Hedgerow pie

To make the pastry, cream together the butter and sugar by hand or using a mixer. Sieve the baking powder and flour together and stir into the butter mix with the salt, then slowly pour in the cream until well mixed. Leave to chill in the refrigerator for about 30 minutes.

Roll the pastry out on a floured table to about 3mm thick. Cut a disc large enough to line an 18 x 3cm deep loose-bottomed tart tin. Cut another disc to fit the top. Lightly grease the tin with butter and line with the larger disc of pastry to just above the top of the tin. Leave to rest for 1 hour in the fridge. Meanwhile, put 200g of the blackberries into a saucepan with the caster sugar and water, bring to a simmer and cook for 3–4 minutes. Mix the arrowroot with a little water, add to the berries and simmer for 2–3 minutes more, stirring occasionally. Strain through a fine meshed sieve into a bowl. Leave to cool a little, then mix with the blackcurrants and remaining blackberries. Preheat the oven to 200°C/gas mark 6.

Remove the pastry from the fridge, line the tart tin with greaseproof paper, fill with baking beans and bake for 10 minutes without colouring. Remove the baking beans and paper from the pastry and leave to cool a little. Spoon the berry mixture almost to the top of the pie shell without overfilling with liquid. Brush the edges of the pastry lid with a little of the beaten egg white, lay over the top and seal the edges by pinching with your fingers.

Brush the lid with more beaten egg white and make a 2cm slit in the centre with a knife (this will allow the steam to escape while cooking). Bake the pie on a tray for 20–25 minutes until golden. Turn the oven down a little or cover the pie with foil if it begins to colour too rapidly. Leave to rest for about 15 minutes before turning out.

Serve dusted with icing sugar and accompanied by a generous spoonful of sour cream.

SERVES 6–8

FOR THE PASTRY

110G SOFT BUTTER

135G CASTER SUGAR

½ TSP BAKING POWDER

225G STRONG WHITE BREAD FLOUR

A PINCH OF SALT

125ML DOUBLE CREAM

FOR THE FILLING

600G BLACKBERRIES, FRESH OR FROZEN

120G CASTER SUGAR

3 TBSP WATER

1 TSP ARROWROOT OR CORNFLOUR

200G BLACKCURRANTS, FRESH OR FROZEN

1 EGG WHITE, BEATEN TOGETHER WITH 1 TBSP CASTER SUGAR

ICING SUGAR, FOR DUSTING

If you are a bit of a forager you probably won't miss the opportunity to make the most of the abundance of blackberries in autumn. This pie is the perfect way to use your harvest, though it is equally good when made with a mixture of other foraged fruits like damsons or elderberries – take your pick.

BISCUITS

Shortbread

Combine the butter and sugar together in a bowl until just mixed but not creamed. Gradually mix in the flour to form a light dough. Cover in cling film and refrigerate for 30–40 minutes. Preheat the oven to 160°C/gas mark 3.

Roll out the dough on a floured work surface to 5mm thick. Cut the shortbread out with a cutter into circles or cut into rectangles or long, straw-like shapes using a knife. Transfer to a non-stick baking tray and scatter with a little extra caster sugar.

Bake for about 8 minutes or until golden. Dust with extra sugar and leave on the baking tray to cool. Store in an airtight container for up to 48 hours.

MAKES 16–20

225G SALTED BUTTER, SOFTENED

120G CASTER SUGAR, PLUS EXTRA FOR DUSTING

300G STRONG WHITE BREAD FLOUR, PLUS EXTRA FOR FLOURING

- -

Simple shortbread makes a good tea-time snack or a great treat to pop in the children's pockets for school. It's also an excellent accompaniment to desserts like fools, possets, ice cream or cranachan – that simple Scottish pudding of raspberries, lightly toasted oats, sugar, whipped cream and whisky. To vary your shortbread, try adding a few chopped nuts to the mix or even some chopped pieces of dark chocolate.

- -

Baklava

Preheat the oven to 180°C/gas mark 4.

Grease a 16–18 x 28cm non-stick baking tray with butter or line with baking parchment. Take a sheet of the filo pastry, place it in the tray and brush with the melted butter. Place a second sheet on top of the first and brush with butter again before repeating with a further 8 sheets of pastry, ensuring you cover the pastry you are not using with a damp cloth to prevent it from drying out.

In a clean bowl, mix together the nuts, sugar and cardamom. Spread three-quarters of the mixture over the pastry in the tray. Layer up the remaining sheets of filo on top of the nut mixture, brushing each sheet with butter as before.

Using the point of a sharp knife, cut a criss-cross pattern into the top layers of the pastry, cutting through into the filling.

Place the baklava in the preheated oven for approximately 20 minutes, then decrease the oven temperature to 150°/gas mark 2 and cook for a further 30–40 minutes, or until the pastry is slightly puffed and golden. Remove from the oven and leave to cool slightly.

To make the syrup, heat the sugar, water, lemon juice and orange blossom water in a small, heavy-bottomed saucepan and simmer over a medium heat for about 15 minutes, until the sugar has melted and the liquid is syrupy.

Pour the syrup into the slits in the baklava, sprinkle over the remaining nut mixture and leave to cool. Cut into strips or small rectangular or square pieces and serve.

MAKES 25–30

225G UNSALTED BUTTER, MELTED, PLUS EXTRA FOR GREASING

18 SHEETS OF FILO PASTRY

225–250G MIXED PISTACHIOS, BLANCHED ALMONDS AND WALNUTS, ROUGHLY CHOPPED

2 TBSP GRANULATED SUGAR

1 TSP GROUND CARDAMOM

FOR THE SYRUP

350G GRANULATED SUGAR

300ML WATER

1 TBSP LEMON JUICE

2 TBSP ORANGE BLOSSOM WATER

- - - - - - - - - - - - - - - - - - - -

I must say I really have to be in the mood
for these Mediterranean biscuits as they are
just so sweet. I do find, though, that once
they are plonked in front of me - especially
with a cup of Turkish coffee - my resistance
waivers. You can vary the nuts in this if
you like, just make sure to use good-quality
ones that haven't got bitter skins.

- - - - - - - - - - - - - - - - - - - -

Arlette biscuits

Roll out the pastry on a work surface dusted with flour and icing sugar as thin as possible. Dust generously with icing sugar, fold in half, dust with more sugar then fold in half again. Roll out with a little more flour and icing sugar and rest in the fridge for an hour.

Remove from the fridge and roll out the pastry as thin as possible (you want to be almost able to see through it). Using a knife or suitably shaped cutter, cut the pastry into rough oval shapes. Delicately transfer the arlettes to a baking tray or the underside of a baking tin with a spatula, reshaping a bit once moved if necessary. Brush with egg white, scatter with the caster sugar and leave to rest in the fridge for 15 minutes.

Preheat the oven to 180°C/gas mark 4.

Bake for about 8–10 minutes until golden, then remove from the oven. Dust with icing sugar and transfer to a wire rack to cool.

MAKES 10–12

200–250G READY-MADE ALL-BUTTER PUFF PASTRY TRIMMINGS

PLAIN FLOUR, FOR DUSTING

150G ICING SUGAR, PLUS EXTRA FOR DUSTING

1 EGG WHITE, TO GLAZE

2 TBSP CASTER SUGAR

Puff pastry trimmings tend to get binned, but I always fold mine up and pop them in the freezer – rolled out wafer-thin with some sugar they make great biscuits to serve with puddings.

Anzac biscuits

Preheat the oven to 160°C/gas mark 3.

Melt the butter and syrup in a large saucepan on a low heat. Dissolve the bicarbonate of soda in the boiling water then stir into the butter mixture.

Mix the remaining ingredients together and stir into the butter mixture.

Using a dessertspoon, place spoonfuls of the mixture on a lightly greased or non-stick baking tray about 4cm apart, to allow for spreading.

Bake for 15–20 minutes, or until a light golden brown. Leave to cool slightly on the tray for a few minutes, then transfer to a wire rack to cool completely. Store in an airtight container until needed.

MAKES 25–30

170G UNSALTED BUTTER, PLUS EXTRA FOR GREASING

1 TBSP GOLDEN SYRUP

1 TSP BICARBONATE OF SODA

1 TBSP BOILING WATER

115G ROLLED OATS

115G PLAIN FLOUR, SIFTED

60G DESSICATED COCONUT

115G CASTER SUGAR

These are traditionally eaten on Anzac day, 25th April, in Australia and New Zealand. They were originally made for the soldiers by their wives during the First World War and were sent over to them in food parcels while they were at the front. Very simple to make, they have a great texture reminiscent of one of my favourite shop-bought biscuits.

Garibaldi biscuits

In a mixing machine, food processor, or a bowl and using your fingers, mix the butter, 95g of the sugar, the flour and salt to form a breadcrumb-like consistency. Add 80g of the chopped raisin mixture, then gradually add the milk and mix together well. Shape into a smooth dough, wrap in cling film and leave to chill in the refrigerator for about 40 minutes.

Meanwhile add the remaining dried fruit to a food processor with the water and blend to a coarse paste. Divide the chilled pastry in two and roll each piece out on silicone or greaseproof paper to make even-sized squares, about 5mm thick. Leave to chill in the refrigerator for a further 30 minutes.

Remove the rolled pastry from the fridge and spread the fruit mixture over one square. Carefully place the other pastry sheet on top. Run the rolling pin over the pastry to make sure it is flat and the fruit is evenly distributed and return to the fridge for another 30 minutes. Preheat the oven to 190°C/gas mark 5.

Cut the pastry square into 10 to 15 rectangular strips. Mix the egg white with 30g of the remaining caster sugar and brush over the pastry. Scatter the rest of the sugar evenly over the top and bake in the oven for 8 minutes, or until golden. Leave to cool and store in an airtight container until required.

MAKES 10–15

95G COLD BUTTER, CUT INTO SMALL PIECES

155G CASTER SUGAR

385G SELF-RAISING FLOUR

A GOOD PINCH OF SALT

250G MIX OF CURRANTS AND RAISINS, FINELY CHOPPED

90ML MILK

3–4 TBSP WATER

1 EGG WHITE, LIGHTLY BEATEN

- -
Remember these? I think they have gone out of fashion but you never know, they may well be back in. Garibaldi are lovely simply with a cuppa and make a great snacking biscuit as well as an excellent accompaniment to ice creams.
- -

Hazelnut and white chocolate cookies

In a food processor or by hand, mix the peanut butter with the sugar until smooth and creamy. Gradually add the beaten egg, mixing together well, then gently fold in the flour with the baking powder and salt to form a smooth dough.

Roll the dough out onto a lightly floured surface to about 1cm thick. Scatter the nuts and chocolate buttons on top and lightly press into the dough. Using a suitable cutter, cut the biscuits into discs, squares or rectangles about 7cm in diameter. Re-roll and cut any excess pastry. Put the cookies onto a non-stick or lightly oiled baking tray and leave to rest in the fridge for about 30 minutes. Preheat the oven to 180°C/gas mark 4.

Bake for 15–20 minutes, then transfer to a cooling rack and leave until cold. Store in an airtight jar or tin.

MAKES ABOUT 12

100G SMOOTH PEANUT BUTTER, SOFTENED

350G LIGHT BROWN SUGAR

4 EGGS, BEATEN

250G PLAIN FLOUR, PLUS EXTRA FOR DUSTING

1 TSP BAKING POWDER

A GOOD PINCH OF SALT

100G SHELLED WEIGHT OF HAZELNUTS, LIGHTLY CRUSHED

200G GOOD-QUALITY WHITE CHOCOLATE BUTTONS

BUTTER, FOR GREASING

- -

If you are into making biscuits, then these are a good alternative to dark chocolate cookies. Get the kids involved in the mixing, rolling and cutting, although they will probably beat you to the biscuit tin once they are cooked.

- -

Ricciarelli

Preheat the oven to 160°C/gas mark 3.

Place the almonds on a tray and roast them for about 15 minutes or so, turning every so often, until golden. Leave to cool, then put in a food processor with half the caster sugar and the lemon zest and blend to a fine consistency.

Clean a stainless steel mixing bowl and a whisk with boiling water and dry with a clean cloth to remove any traces of grease. Whisk the egg whites until stiff, then add the remaining sugar and continue beating until they are stiff and shiny. Fold in the ground almond mixture with the vanilla and almond extracts.

Line a baking tray with silicone or baking paper. Using your fingers, take about half a dessertspoon of the mixture at a time and roll into balls, flattening each lightly until they are about 1cm thick. (Alternatively, pipe them in a piping bag with a plain nozzle.) Arrange the biscuits on the baking tray about 3cm apart.

Bake for about 20–30 minutes, or until golden. Leave to cool on the tray, then remove and dust with icing sugar. Store in an airtight container until needed.

MAKES 20–25

300G WHOLE ALMONDS

225G CASTER SUGAR

ZEST OF ½ A LEMON

2 LARGE EGG WHITES

A FEW DROPS OF GOOD-QUALITY VANILLA EXTRACT

A FEW DROPS OF ALMOND EXTRACT

ICING SUGAR, FOR DUSTING

- -

These are those delicious little biscuits that you commonly see piled up in cafés around Italy, especially in Siena. Like most little biscuits, these are great to just have around to enjoy with tea or coffee, or to take to work as a snack.

- -

Poppy seed and lemon biscuits

Mix the icing sugar, butter, lemon zest, vanilla extract and salt together in a mixer on a low speed for 30 seconds or so, then turn the speed up a little and mix for another 30 seconds. Slowly add the egg white until mixed well, then remove from the machine and fold in the flour and poppy seeds by hand. Preheat the oven to 180°C/gas mark 4.

Place the plastic template decribed below onto a non-stick baking tray or a tray lined with silicone paper. Using a palette knife or spatula, spread a thin layer of the mixture into the cut-out part of the template. Carefully remove the template and repeat with the rest of the mixture.

Bake for about 6–7 minutes or until lightly golden, then remove from the oven. If you want to shape the biscuits, then remove them from the tray with a palette knife while they are still warm and wrap them around a rolling pin or bottle until they cool down and crisp up. (Try rolling them around a sharpening steel or something similar to get cigarette shapes, if you wish.) Store in an airtight container in a dry place for up to 48 hours.

MAKES ABOUT 20

100G ICING SUGAR

100G SOFT BUTTER

FINELY GRATED ZEST OF 1 LEMON

A FEW DROPS OF VANILLA EXTRACT

A PINCH OF SALT

2 SMALL EGG WHITES, LIGHTLY WHISKED

100G PLAIN FLOUR

1 TBSP POPPY SEEDS

- -

These delicate biscuits are perfect for serving with ice cream or sorbet. I find the best way to spread these onto a tray is to use a template made from an old ice cream or plastic container lid. Simply take your lid and cut out a rectangle about 15cm long, leaving a little extra thumb-sized piece at the end to hold while spreading. Now cut out the centre of the rectangle about 1cm from the edge and you'll be left with a great template for spreading these kinds of biscuit mixes.

- -

Sea biscuits

Crumble the seaweed in your hands or briefly give it a whiz in a food processor until sugar-like in consistency.

Put the flour, butter, two-thirds of the salt, black pepper and sugar into a bowl and rub between your fingers to a breadcrumb-like consistency. Add the seaweed and chives and mix together well, then slowly add the water to form a smooth dough.

Roll the dough out onto a lightly floured surface to about 5mm thick. Cut into 5cm squares. Lay on a non-stick or lightly greased baking tray a couple of centimetres apart, transfer to the refrigerator and leave to chill for 2–3 hours.

Preheat the oven to 180°C/gas mark 4.

Sprinkle the biscuits generously with the remaining sea salt and bake for 20–25 minutes, or until golden. Transfer to a wire rack to cool and store in an airtight container for up to a week.

MAKES ABOUT 20

2 SHEETS OF NORI SEAWEED

320G PLAIN FLOUR, PLUS EXTRA FOR DUSTING

200G UNSALTED BUTTER, CHILLED AND DICED

1 TBSP CORNISH SEA SALT

1 TSP FRESHLY GROUND BLACK PEPPER

1 TSP CASTER SUGAR

2 TBSP CHOPPED CHIVES OR GARLIC CHIVES

1–2 TBSP WATER

These are perfect biscuits to nibble with drinks or to serve with cheese. They also make a great canapé base for something fishy like smoked salmon, fish tartare or pâté.

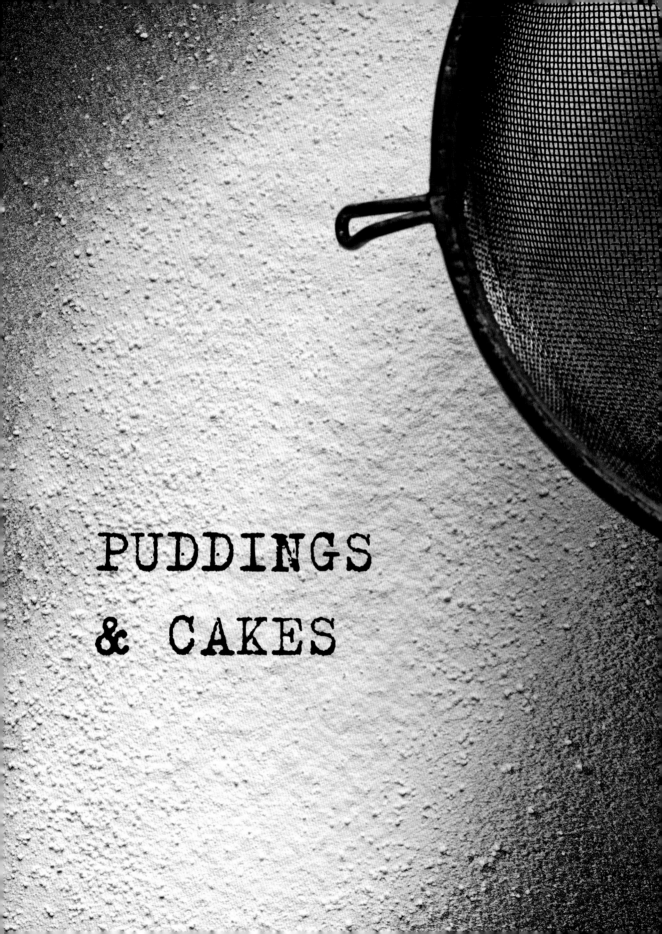

PUDDINGS & CAKES

Baked peaches with Amaretto

Preheat the oven to 180°C/gas mark 4.

Lay the peaches cut-side up on a baking tray. Spoon over two-thirds of the butter and the Amaretto.

Bake in the oven for 15–20 minutes (you may need a little longer if the peaches aren't that ripe), covering them with foil if they are colouring too rapidly. Mix the remaining butter with the Amaretti biscuits in a bowl. Remove the peaches from the oven, spoon over the biscuit mixture and bake for a further 8–10 minutes, until the topping is golden.

To finish, transfer the peaches to serving plates, add the honey and a few tablespoons of water to the cooking tray and simmer for 30 seconds or so, stirring, until well mixed. Spoon the sauce around the peaches and serve with custard, ice cream or mascarpone.

SERVES 4

6 PEACHES OR NECTARINES, HALVED AND THE STONES REMOVED

80G BUTTER, MELTED

100–150ML AMARETTO

120G AMARETTI BISCUITS, COARSELY CRUSHED

2 TBSP CLEAR HONEY

When peaches or nectarines are plentiful this is a great way to make good use of them and give them a different flavour, rather like when you roast vegetables. It also works well with unripe fruit.

Cherry Yorkshire pudding

Preheat the oven to 200°C/gas mark 6.

Place all the ingredients except the cherries in a bowl or a small electric whisker and whisk to form a light batter. Lightly grease 4 individual deep Yorkshire pudding tins and put them in the oven for 5 minutes.

Remove the tins from the oven, divide the cherries between them and add enough batter to half fill each tin. Return to the oven and cook for 15–20 minutes, until the batter has risen and is golden.

Serve with cherry ice cream.

SERVES 4

3 EGGS

100G PLAIN FLOUR

200ML MILK

15G ICING SUGAR

THE SEEDS FROM HALF A VANILLA POD, OR A FEW DROPS OF VANILLA EXTRACT

24 CHERRIES, STONED

- -

Yorkshire puddings - so I've heard but never actually witnessed - often get dished up as a pudding up North. Well, our native Yorkshire pudding is a kind of clafoutis, I suppose, so why not serve it as a dessert? When cherries aren't in season, try using cherries preserved in eau-de-vie to give the puddings a nice kick.

- -

Caramelised oranges

Preheat the oven to 180°C/gas mark 4.

Cut the oranges and blood oranges, if using, horizontally into 2cm slices.

Put the honey and butter on a baking tray that will fit the orange pieces snugly. Heat in the oven for about 10 minutes, giving the occasional stir, until the butter starts bubbling. Add the oranges and kumquat pieces and cook for 15 minutes, turning during cooking. Add the satsumas and cook for another 7–8 minutes until caramelised, then remove from the oven. Drain off the liquid into a saucepan, add the Cointreau and simmer for a few minutes until reduced by a third. Pour the sauce back over the oranges and leave to cool slightly.

Serve warm either with ice cream or crème fraîche. These caramelised oranges would also make a great accompaniment to the flourless orange cake on page 176.

SERVES 4–6

4 LARGE ORANGES, PEELED
(OR 2 LARGE ORANGES AND 2
BLOOD ORANGES)

120G HONEY

120G BUTTER

16 KUMQUATS, HALVED

4 SATSUMAS, CLEMENTINES OR
MANDARINS, PEELED AND
SEGMENTED

100ML COINTREAU

This is a take on those bowls of oranges with caramel sauce that used to appear on sweet trollies next to the profiteroles and cheesecake. They were never something that really appealed to me, maybe because they often looked a bit like an afterthought. I've tried to make those dull orange bowls a bit more sexy here, using a selection of different oranges along with a kick of Cointreau.

Profiteroles

Put the milk, water, butter, salt and sugar into a saucepan and bring to the boil. Remove from the heat, mix in the flour and stir with a wooden spoon or spatula until smooth. Return the pan to a low heat and stir for about a minute until the mixture leaves the sides of the pan. Transfer to a bowl.

Gradually whisk the beaten eggs into the mix a little at a time, until the mixture is smooth and shiny. Preheat the oven to 180°C/gas mark 4.

Take a non-stick baking tray or line a baking tray with baking parchment. Load the choux pastry into a piping bag and pipe small or large rounds onto the tray 3–4cm apart. (For éclairs, just pipe the mixture into short or long straight lines about 6–8cm thick using a 2cm nozzle.) Brush the tops with the egg yolk mixture and bake for between 10–20 minutes depending on the size, or until the profiteroles are golden and crisp. Remove from the oven, leave to cool a little and transfer to a cooling rack.

To make the filling, whisk together the cream, vanilla extract and sugar by hand or using a mixing machine, until fairly stiff. Load the cream mixture into a piping bag, make a hole in the base of your profiteroles and pipe in. Serve as they are or with ice cream and chocolate sauce (see page 183).

MAKES 20–25 LARGE OR 40–50 SMALL PROFITEROLES

125ML MILK

125ML WATER

100G BUTTER, DICED

½ TSP SALT

1 TSP CASTER SUGAR

150G PLAIN FLOUR

4 EGGS, BEATEN

1 EGG YOLK BEATEN TOGETHER WITH 1 TBSP MILK, TO GLAZE

FOR THE FILLING

250ML DOUBLE OR WHIPPING CREAM

A FEW DROPS OF VANILLA EXTRACT

60G CASTER SUGAR

Profiteroles seem to have vanished from restaurant menus. This seems to me to be a shame, as a profiterole that oozes cream when you bite into it is a wonderful thing (especially when served with hot chocolate sauce). You can serve them just like this or make the dish a little more indulgent by adding some ice cream and scattering over the profiteroles some lightly toasted, sugared nuts like almonds or pistachios.

Pineapple upside-down cake

Take 6 individual round tart tins about 3–4cm deep. Melt 80g of the butter and mix together with 80g of the caster sugar in a small bowl. Brush half this mixture over the sides and base of the tin.

Heat the remaining melted butter mixture in a frying pan until it begins to bubble. Add the pineapple slices and cook over a medium to high heat, turning every so often, until they begin to colour. Remove from the heat. Place a pineapple ring and a tablespoon of the cooking liquid in each tin, reserving any excess. Preheat the oven to 175°C/gas mark 4.

Put the remaining butter and sugar, the eggs, self-raising flour, baking powder and hazelnuts in a food processor and mix together for a minute or so until smooth. Pour the mixture evenly into the tins and cook for 30–40 minutes, until golden. Leave to cool a little, run a knife around the edge of each tin and turn out onto warmed serving plates. Spoon over any excess cooking liquid and serve either hot or warm with thick cream or crème fraîche.

SERVES 6

330G BUTTER, SOFTENED

330G CASTER SUGAR

1 SMALL PINEAPPLE, PEELED, CORED AND CUT INTO 2CM RINGS

4 LARGE EGGS

200G SELF-RAISING FLOUR

2 TSP BAKING POWDER

50G GROUND HAZELNUTS

- -

My introduction to proper cooking came when I opted for domestic science in the fifth year at school instead of technology. I loved woodwork, but found metalwork painfully dull. Filing away at a piece of metal for four weeks seemed a dreary way to get a key ring. That was when, for the first time in history, boys could do domestic science instead of another subject. Only four of us joined Miss Bell, a young Delia lookalike, for cookery lessons, but we had a bit of a laugh. Our first achievement was pineapple upside-down cake.

- -

Rum baba

Sift the flour and salt into a bowl and make a well in the centre. Add the dissolved yeast mixture, eggs and sugar. With floured hands, mix everything to combine and knead for a couple of minutes in the bowl until you have a smooth, elastic dough.

Dot the top of the dough with the butter, cover with a damp tea towel and leave in a warm place for about an hour, until the mixture has doubled in volume. Again with floured hands, knead the butter into the dough for a minute or so until it becomes smooth and glossy.

Butter 8 dariole or similar moulds and chill them in the freezer for 10–15 minutes before buttering a second time. Spoon the mixture into the moulds until two-thirds full. Place the moulds on a tray, cover and leave to prove for 20 minutes, until the mixture has risen to the top of the moulds. Preheat the oven to 200°C/gas mark 6.

Bake the babas for about 15–20 minutes or until golden. Carefully turn them out (using a small knife if you need to) and transfer to a cooling tray.

In a large saucepan, dissolve the sugar in the water and boil rapidly for a few minutes to make a clear syrup. Stir in the rum, then add the babas, leaving them to soak for about 5–10 minutes and turning them with a spoon every so often so they absorb as much of the liquid as possible. Transfer to a serving dish and serve with sweetened whipped or thick cream and a jug of rum for pouring over.

SERVES 8

225G PLAIN FLOUR

1 TSP SALT

2 TSP DRIED YEAST, DISSOLVED IN 3 TBSP WARM WATER

3 MEDIUM EGGS, BEATEN

1 TBSP CASTER SUGAR

100G BUTTER, SOFTENED, IN KNOBS, PLUS A LITTLE EXTRA FOR GREASING THE MOULDS

FOR THE SYRUP

500G GRANULATED SUGAR

800ML WATER

200ML GOOD-QUALITY RUM

- -

This is another of those old sweet trolley classics that you rarely see these days, though I'm not sure why it's faded away as, when it's made well, it's a top notch dessert. I've been to restaurants where I've ordered this, and a bottle of rum gets plonked on the table, which is a great touch if you want to indulge that little bit more!

- -

St Clements cheesecake

To make the pastry, put the butter, icing sugar, and salt in a bowl, mix to combine, then slowly add the egg yolks. Gradually mix in the flour to form a smooth dough. Shape into a ball, wrap in cling film and leave to chill in the refrigerator for 30 minutes.

Butter a 20 x 4cm deep loose-bottomed flan tin. Roll out the pastry on a floured work surface to a large circle, 3–4mm thick. Use to line the tin, leaving the edges untrimmed, with any excess pastry being used to patch up any holes or cracks. Refrigerate for a further 30 minutes. Preheat the oven to 160°C/gas mark 3.

Prick the base of the pastry case all over with a fork. Line the case with greaseproof paper, fill with baking beans and bake for 30 minutes. Remove the beans and paper and return to the oven for 5 minutes until lightly golden, then remove from the oven and leave to cool. Lower the oven to 150°C/gas mark 2.

Meantime, make the filling. Combine the fromage frais, curd cheese, sour cream and sugar in a bowl and mix together thoroughly. In another bowl, whisk the eggs until frothy, then gently fold into the cheese mixture. Stir in the orange and lemon juice and zest.

Pour the filling into the pastry case and bake for 1¼–1½ hours. Check the filling is cooked by inserting a skewer into the centre – when removed it should be clean. Leave to cool on a wire rack for about 30 minutes before removing from the flan tin. To finish, warm the marmalade in a pan and strain through a sieve. Spoon over the cheesecake before serving.

SERVES 8

FOR THE PASTRY

200G BUTTER, CUT INTO SMALL PIECES AND SLIGHTLY SOFTENED, PLUS EXTRA FOR GREASING

100G ICING SUGAR

A GOOD PINCH OF TABLE SALT

2 EGG YOLKS

250G PLAIN FLOUR

FOR THE FILLING

350G FROMAGE FRAIS

350G CURD CHEESE

150G SOUR CREAM

175G CASTER SUGAR

4 EGGS

FINELY GRATED ZEST AND JUICE OF 3 ORANGES

FINELY GRATED ZEST AND JUICE OF 2 LEMONS

TO SERVE

150G ORANGE MARMALADE

- -

As a kid I always used to drink St Clements at the golf club, and love the combination of orange and lemon to this day. There are all sorts of sweet and savoury dishes that use it, but I especially like it in this cheesecake with its shortcake-like base. If you can't find curd cheese then simply double the quantity of fromage frais.

- -

Saffron and olive oil cake

Preheat the oven to 180°C/gas mark 4. Lightly oil a round 18–20 x 6–8cm deep, loose-bottomed cake tin and line with greaseproof paper.

Put the saffron-infused milk, eggs and sugar in a mixing bowl and whisk until light, fluffy and doubled in volume. Slowly pour in the olive oil, stirring, then fold in the flour with a spoon until well mixed. Pour the mixture into the cake tin.

Bake for about 25–30 minutes, testing by inserting a skewer or the point of a small knife in the centre – if it comes out clean, it's done. Leave to cool for 15 minutes, then remove from the tin and transfer to a cooling rack. Serve on its own or with crème fraîche or mascarpone.

MAKES 1 MEDIUM CAKE

175ML VIRGIN OLIVE OIL (PREFERABLY NOT TOO STRONG), PLUS EXTRA FOR OILING

A COUPLE OF GOOD PINCHES OF SAFFRON STRANDS, SOAKED IN 2 TBSP MILK OVERNIGHT

3 MEDIUM EGGS, BEATEN

175G CASTER SUGAR

175G SELF-RAISING FLOUR

Olive oil, instead of butter, is used for baking in Mediterranean countries where there are a lot more olive trees than dairy cattle. If your cholesterol is a tad high as well, then olive oil is a perfect substitute, so you don't need to feel too guilty about snacking on cake.

Flourless orange cake

Place the clean, whole and unpeeled oranges in a pan with enough water to cover. Bring to the boil, cover with a lid and simmer for about 1½ hours or until soft, adding more water if necessary. (You can do this in a pressure cooker in half the time – just half cover the fruit with water.) Drain the oranges and cut into quarters, discarding any major pips. Put the orange pieces, including peel, in the food processor and blend to a pulp. Leave to cool.

Preheat the oven to 180°C/gas mark 4. Lightly oil and line a rectangular loaf tin or 23cm round loose-bottomed cake tin with greaseproof paper.

Beat the egg yolks and sugar together in a large bowl until light and fluffy, Beat in the orange pulp, almonds, and baking powder. In a separate bowl, beat the egg whites until they form soft peaks, then fold gently into the orange mixture. Spoon the mixture into the tin.

Bake for an hour, until golden and firm to the touch. Turn out carefully and store in an airtight container until needed.

SERVES 6–8

2 MEDIUM ORANGES

3 EGGS, SEPARATED

120G CASTER SUGAR

150G GROUND ALMONDS

½ TSP BAKING POWDER

This is a pretty easy, delicate and very moist cake, which gets demolished in no time when I make it and is great for anyone with a wheat intolerance. Serve as an afternoon or anytime tea cake, or as a dessert with caramelised oranges (p167) and ice cream or crème fraîche.

Somerset apple cake

Prepare a loose-bottomed 24 x 6–8cm deep cake tin by greasing it lightly and lining with greaseproof paper. Melt 60g of the butter and pour over the base, scatter over the demerara sugar evenly and layer over the apple slices until the base is covered.

Preheat the oven to 160°C/gas mark 3.

Cream the remaining butter and brown sugar together in a bowl until light and fluffy. Gradually beat in the eggs and honey. Gently fold in the flour and mixed spice, then stir in the Pomona and the cooking apples. Transfer to the cake tin and bake for 1¼ hours, or until a skewer inserted into the centre of the cake comes out clean. Cool in the tin for 15 minutes, then turn out and serve warm on its own or with thick cream.

MAKES 1 MEDIUM CAKE

230G UNSALTED BUTTER, SOFTENED, PLUS EXTRA FOR GREASING

2 TBSP DEMERARA SUGAR

3 EATING APPLES, PEELED, CORED AND SLICED

170G SOFT BROWN SUGAR

3 MEDIUM EGGS, BEATEN

1 TBSP HONEY

240G SELF-RAISING FLOUR, SIFTED

1 TSP MIXED SPICE

80ML POMONA OR KINGSTON BLACK

600–700G COOKING APPLES, PEELED, CORED AND CUT INTO SMALLISH CHUNKS

All the apple-growing regions of the UK have their own versions of this cake. This is ideal to serve as a dessert with ice cream, clotted or thick cream. I've used Pomona or Kingston Black here which are apple liqueurs made by Julian Temperley in Somerset. If you can't get hold of either of these, simmer 250ml of cider until reduced to 80ml and use this instead.

Wheat-free chocolate and Guinness cake

Preheat the oven to 180°C/gas mark 4. Butter and line a 24 x 6–8cm deep cake tin with greaseproof paper.

Cream the butter and sugar together in a bowl until light and fluffy, then gradually add the beaten eggs.

Mix together the Guiness and cocoa in a separate mixing bowl, then add the grated chocolate. Gradually add to the cake mixture alternately with the flour, stirring between each addition until completely mixed.

Pour the cake mix into the cake tin and bake for 1–1¼ hours, or until a skewer inserted into the centre of the cake comes out clean. You may need to cover the cake with foil or greaseproof paper after about 30–45 minutes to prevent the top from browning.

Remove from the oven and leave to stand for 10 minutes before turning out onto a wire rack to cool.

MAKES 1 MEDIUM CAKE

225G BUTTER, PLUS EXTRA FOR GREASING

350G SOFT DARK BROWN SUGAR

4 EGGS, BEATEN

400ML GUINNESS

100G GOOD-QUALITY COCOA POWDER

150G DARK CHOCOLATE (60% COCOA), GRATED

225G DOVE'S FARM SELF-RAISING FLOUR

- - - - - - - - - - - - - - - -
A lovely rich cake that isn't overly
sweet because of the Guinness. I've
made it with wheat-free self-raising
flour so that it's suitable for those
with wheat allergies who still crave
a little something sweet!
- - - - - - - - - - - - - - - -

Ronnie's chocolate cake

Preheat the oven to 180°C/gas mark 4. Lightly grease a 25 x 8cm deep round cake tin and line it with greaseproof paper or baking parchment.

To make the sponge, whisk 250g of the sugar with the egg yolks until pale and fluffy. In a separate bowl, whisk the rest of the sugar with the egg whites until light and fluffy. Sieve the flour and cocoa powder together and gently fold into the egg yolk mixture with the almonds, then fold into the egg white mixture. Pour into the tin and bake in the oven for 25–30 minutes. Check it's cooked by inserting a skewer into the centre – if it comes out clean it's done. Remove from the oven and leave to cool for 15 minutes before turning onto a wire rack.

To make the syrup, bring the water and sugar to the boil, leave to cool and mix in the Amaretto.

To make the filling, melt the chocolate in a bowl over a pan of simmering water, then stir in the softened butter and remove from the heat. Meanwhile, whisk the eggs, yolks and sugar until doubled in volume. Carefully fold the two mixes together.

To make the glaze, bring the cream, milk, glucose and oil to the boil. Pour over the chopped chocolate and stir until melted.

Adjust the oven to 110°C/gas mark ¼. Clean the cake tin and grease and line it as before. Cut the cooled cake horizontally into four discs. Lay the first disc back in the bottom of the tin, pour over a quarter of the syrup then spoon over a quarter of the filling. Repeat this layering with the remaining sponge discs, filling and syrup, finishing with the last of the filling. Level the top and bake for about 20 minutes or until just set. Remove from the oven and leave to cool.

Remove the cake from the tin and place on a wire rack. Pour the chocolate glaze over and spread evenly across the top and sides. Set in the fridge. Serve at room temperature.

SERVES 10–12

BUTTER, FOR GREASING

500G CASTER SUGAR, PLUS A LITTLE EXTRA FOR DUSTING

6 EGGS, SEPARATED

100G STRONG WHITE BREAD FLOUR

50G GOOD-QUALITY COCOA POWDER

100G GROUND ALMONDS

FOR THE SYRUP

50ML WATER

50G GRANULATED SUGAR

75ML AMARETTO OR CRÈME DE CACAO

FOR THE FILLING

300G DARK CHOCOLATE (60% COCOA), CHOPPED

200G BUTTER, SOFTENED

6 EGGS, PLUS 4 EGG YOLKS

60G CASTER SUGAR

FOR THE CHOCOLATE GLAZE

250ML DOUBLE CREAM

125ML MILK

25G GLUCOSE

25ML OLIVE OIL

600G GOOD-QUALITY DARK CHOCOLATE (60% COCOA), CHOPPED

- -

When we opened our restaurant in Selfridges, London, I wanted to serve a chocolate cake that was memorable without looking too fussily over-the-top. My group pastry chef Ronnie came up with this rich concoction that fitted the bill nicely. It may look a little long-winded but it's well worth the effort.

- -

Chocolate and almond pavlova

First make the meringue. Preheat the oven to 120°C/gas mark 1. Clean a stainless steel mixing bowl and a whisk (preferably electric) with boiling water and dry with a clean cloth to remove any traces of grease. Whisk the egg whites until stiff, then add the sugar and continue whisking until shiny. Add the cornflour and vinegar and whisk for a further 45 seconds or so.

Spoon the meringue mixture into a long, rough slipper shape on a clean baking tray lined with silicone or greaseproof paper. Cook in the oven for 1½–2 hours, or until the meringue is crisp but not coloured on the outside and soft in the very middle (you may need to cook it a little longer depending on your oven). Remove and leave to cool.

To make the chocolate sauce, put the chocolate buttons in a bowl, bring the cream and milk to the boil and pour over the chocolate, stirring, until the chocolate has melted.

To serve, hollow out the pavlova a little by carefully pushing the centre in with the back of a spoon. Using a serving spoon or ice cream scoop, spoon the ice cream into the hollow. Pour over the sauce and scatter over the almonds and chocolate shavings to finish.

SERVES 6–8

4 EGG WHITES

140G CASTER SUGAR

½ TSP CORNFLOUR

½ TSP WHITE WINE VINEGAR

FOR THE CHOCOLATE SAUCE

150G DARK CHOCOLATE BUTTONS

150ML DOUBLE CREAM

50ML MILK

TO SERVE

6–8 SCOOPS OF VANILLA ICE CREAM

60G FLAKED OR WHOLE BLANCHED ALMONDS LIGHTLY TOASTED WITH ½ TBSP ICING SUGAR

100G MIX OF DARK AND WHITE CHOCOLATE SHAVINGS

- -

I often serve this for big dinner parties, doubling the recipe and putting two of these great looking slipper-shaped meringues down in the middle of the table to share. You can vary this depending on how much time you have on your hands and can use chocolate mousse, crème fraîche or chocolate ice cream in place of the vanilla. You can make your own chocolate shavings for decorating by just pulling the blade of a knife across the flat side of a block of chocolate.

- -

Baked Alaska

Remove the ice cream and sorbet from the freezer about 10 minutes before you assemble the Alaska. Put the water and caster sugar in a pan and bring to the boil. Remove from the heat and leave to cool a little, then add 40ml of the eau-de-vie.

Cut the sponge horizontally into three discs, about 8mm thick. Put one disc onto an oven-proof serving dish and brush it generously with the sugar syrup. Spread the ice cream over the sponge, leaving a 2cm margin around the edge. Spread the sorbet over the middle of the ice cream, leaving 2cm of ice cream at the edge. Put it into the freezer for about 30–40 minutes, until firm.

Cut the two remaining slices of sponge in half, then cut three of the halves in half again. Using a 10cm cutter or a sharp knife, cut the remaining half into a circle. Remove the Alaska from the freezer and place the sponge disc in the middle of the sorbet. Place the quarter pieces around the sorbet and ice cream to cover, butting up against the disc in the middle to form a dome. Brush the top of the sponge generously with the sugar syrup and return it to the freezer.

Meantime, make the meringue. In a mixing machine or by hand, whisk the egg whites until stiff. Add the caster sugar and continue whisking until they are really stiff and shiny, about 3–4 minutes.

Remove the Alaska from the freezer. Either cover the ice cream with the meringue using a palette knife or spatula to give a rough, natural effect or load it into a piping bag with a star or plain nozzle and pipe it from the centre down to the edge until covered. Return to the freezer until required.

Preheat the oven to 200°C/gas mark 6. Bake the Alaska for 5–6 minutes until it is lightly coloured. Meantime, heat the remaining eau-de-vie in a pan over a low heat. Take the Alaska to the table. Carefully light the eau-de-vie with a match and pour it over the Alaska, allowing the flames to burn out before serving with a handful or two of fresh raspberries.

SERVES 4–6

200G VANILLA ICE CREAM

200G RASPBERRY SORBET OR ICE CREAM

100ML WATER

100G CASTER SUGAR

100ML RASPBERRY EAU-DE-VIE

12–14CM ROUND SPONGE CAKE

FOR THE MERINGUE

3 EGG WHITES

100G CASTER SUGAR

- -

This impressive looking dinner party dessert seems complicated, but buying the ice cream and sponge will allow you to get away with murder as far as your guests are concerned. Try varying the ice cream and fruit filling according to the season or personal preferences – in winter you could used preserved fruits like cherries steeped in brandy, for example.

- -

Index

Z

I'd like to thank all those who have worked on this book. Thanks to Jo Harris, for her help vetting the flourless recipes and to Ronnie Murray for help recipe testing and for that superb chocolate cake. Many thanks to Quadrille Publishing, especially to Jane O'Shea and the team who helped put the book together: photographer Jason Lowe, designer Lawrence Morton and editor Simon Davis.

Editorial Director Jane O'Shea
Creative Director Helen Lewis
Project Editor Simon Davis
Art Direction & Design Lawrence Morton
Photographer Jason Lowe
Production Director Vincent Smith
Production Controller James Finan

First published in 2012 by
Quadrille Publishing Limited
Alhambra House
27–31 Charing Cross Road
London WC2H 0LS
www.quadrille.co.uk

Text © 2012 Mark Hix
Photography © 2012 Jason Lowe
Design and layout © 2012 Quadrille Publishing Ltd

Cataloguing in Publication Data: a catalogue record for this book is available from the British Library.

ISBN 978 184949 124 2

Printed in China